T0311733

Cambridge Elements ≡

Elements in the Global Middle Ages
edited by
Geraldine Heng
University of Texas at Austin
Susan Noakes
University of Minnesota, Twin Cities

EURASIAN MUSICAL JOURNEYS

Five Tales

Gabriela Currie
University of Minnesota, Twin Cities
Lars Christensen
University of Minnesota, Twin Cities

CAMBRIDGE
UNIVERSITY PRESS

CAMBRIDGE
UNIVERSITY PRESS

University Printing House, Cambridge CB2 8BS, United Kingdom

One Liberty Plaza, 20th Floor, New York, NY 10006, USA

477 Williamstown Road, Port Melbourne, VIC 3207, Australia

314–321, 3rd Floor, Plot 3, Splendor Forum, Jasola District Centre,
New Delhi – 110025, India

103 Penang Road, #05–06/07, Visioncrest Commercial, Singapore 238467

Cambridge University Press is part of the University of Cambridge.

It furthers the University's mission by disseminating knowledge in the pursuit of
education, learning, and research at the highest international levels of excellence.

www.cambridge.org
Information on this title: www.cambridge.org/9781108823296
DOI: 10.1017/9781108913805

© Gabriela Currie and Lars Christensen 2022

This publication is in copyright. Subject to statutory exception
and to the provisions of relevant collective licensing agreements,
no reproduction of any part may take place without the written
permission of Cambridge University Press.

First published 2022

A catalogue record for this publication is available from the British Library.

ISBN 978-1-108-82329-6 Paperback
ISSN 2632-3427 (online)
ISSN 2632-3419 (print)

Cambridge University Press has no responsibility for the persistence or accuracy of
URLs for external or third-party internet websites referred to in this publication
and does not guarantee that any content on such websites is, or will remain,
accurate or appropriate.

Eurasian Musical Journeys

Five Tales

Elements in the Global Middle Ages

DOI: 10.1017/9781108913805
First published online: April 2022

Gabriela Currie
University of Minnesota

Lars Christensen
University of Minnesota

Author for correspondence: Gabriela Currie, ilnit001@umn.edu

Abstract: This Element explores the circulation of musical instruments, practices, and thought in premodern Eurasia at the crossroads of empires and nomadic cultures. It takes into consideration mechanisms of transmission, appropriation, adaptation, and integration that helped shape musical traditions that are perceived as culturally and geographically distinct yet are historically linked. The five stories featured here range from the geographically diverse performing groups during the Sui and Tang era, to the elusive musical world of Kucha in the Tarim Basin; from the fragmentary history of a single instrument linked to the Turkic peoples across Eurasia, to the transcontinental circulation of sound-making automata, including the organ, on both east–west and north–south axes. Within the conceptual background of cultural encounter and exchange, this Element provides possible strategies for integrating such information into the historical tapestry of Eurasian transcontinental networks as explored in other Elements in the series.

Keywords: musical instruments, Silk Road, Central Asia, music, cultural commerce

© Gabriela Currie and Lars Christensen 2022

ISBNs: 9781108823296 (PB), 9781108913805 (OC)
ISSNs: 2632-3427 (online), 2632-3419 (print)

Contents

1 Prologue

One of the most exquisite musical instruments is the five-string lute known as the Raden Shitan no Gogen Biwa 螺鈿紫檀五絃琵琶 ("mother-of-pearl inlay red sandalwood five-string lute"; hereafter the Gogen Biwa), today in the Shōsōin collection in Nara, Japan (Figure 1). The instrument, the only extant example of its type from premodern Eurasia, was apparently received by Emperor Shōmu before his death in 756, upon which it was placed in the collection at Shōsōin, a specially constructed storehouse in the Tōdai-ji temple complex in the then-capital Nara. The 9,000 or so items in the collection, including several other musical instruments, are not accessible except by the personal permission of the emperor, though certain items are put on display every year to great historical interest.

Given its status as regalia within the world's longest continuous imperial line, one might expect that these sacred objects were of ancient Japanese provenance. Indeed, during the apogee of Imperial Japan, the Japanese provenance of many of the finest items in the Shōsōin was the standard view (Watson 1979: 167). Yet, the image inlaid on the front of the Gogen Biwa betrays a larger story, one that places this musical object at the crossroads of Eurasian cultural encounters. The musician playing a four-string lute astride a Bactrian camel is a motif fairly typical of the art from the Tang Empire, in particular the so-called "three-color" (*sancai* 三彩) lead-glazed burial ceramics.[1]

Japan's closest international relationship in the eighth century was with the Tang Empire, and there is reason to suspect that the Gogen Biwa was manufactured there and probably connected with the court music of Chang'an (modern Xi'an), the Tang capital. As Naitō Sakae recently argued, the instrument may have been commissioned there and brought to Japan sometime before 735 by Kibi no Makibi 吉備真備 (695–775), a ranking member of the Japanese embassy sent to the Tang court in 716. It would likely have been presented to Emperor Shōmu during the festivities that marked the return of the embassy and featured performances of Tang and Silla (Korean) music (cited in Hu 2017: 186).

This was not the sole Japanese musical encounter with the Tang. Several other of the numerous Japanese missions to the Tang court during the seventh and eighth centuries were known to have focused on cultural aspects, including music and dance (Picken & Nickson 1997: 2). Instruments and performance practices were passed to Japan from these missions, where they were known as "Tang music" (*Tōgaku* 唐樂) repertoire. *Tōgaku* combined with indigenous and other exogenous musical traditions (for instance, that of the aforementioned

---

[1] For example, https://sogdians.si.edu/camel-with-musicians/.

(a)   (b)

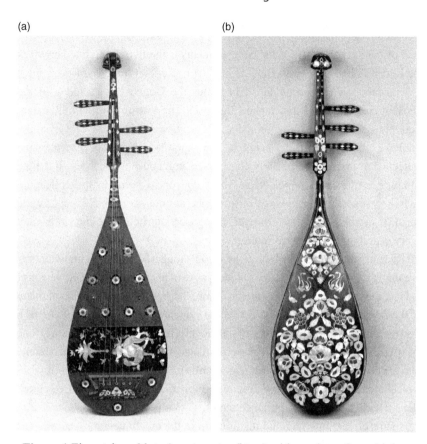

Figure 1 Five-stringed lute (*wuxian pipa/biwa*) with mother-of-pearl inlay. Meiji era, nineteenth century. Copied from the original Gogen Biwa of the Nara period, eighth century, in the Shōsōin Repository, Nara. Tokyo National Museum H-1090. Source: ColBase: Integrated Collections Database of the National Institutes for Cultural Heritage, Japan (https://colbase.nich.go.jp/col lection_items/tnm/H-1090?locale=en).

Silla) to form the musical style known as *gagaku*, a Japanese rendering of the Chinese term *yayue* 雅樂, meaning "elegant music." *Gagaku* survives as a living tradition in Japan, still performed by a hereditary group of musicians in ensembles that include instruments recognizably descended from court ensembles in Chang'an. There is even a connection in notation: a very early score for four-string lute preserved in the Shōsōin collection matches quite closely the tablature system used in three manuscripts preserved in a cave in Dunhuang, a site over 1,500 km west of Chang'an that served as an important node in the musical and artistic Eurasian network.

These and many other objects in the Shōsōin reflect Japan's position as the eastern terminus of what is usually called the Silk Road. "Silk Road" (*Seidenstrasse*), a term commonly attributed to Ferdinand Freiherr von Richthofen (1833–1905), was used by German orientalists in the nineteenth century to describe what they imagined primarily as a link between Rome and China (Mertens 2019). Its namesake commodity was already popular in Rome at the time of Julius Caesar, and the word "silk" itself might very well be one of few words borrowed from Chinese into an Indo-European language (Wang 1993). However, we now know the Silk Road was never a single road but a network of land trade routes with numerous intersecting branches; very few people traveled along its entire length, with trade instead taking place on short-distance segments, and there were many branches whose main commonality was avoiding impassable mountains and deserts. While silk and other East Asian goods were also frequently exported by sea, overland back-and-forth trade facilitated the accretion of items from the numerous other cultures the Silk Roads passed through. While merchants were motivated by profits, religious adherents to Buddhism, Christianity, Manichaeism, Zoroastrianism, and Islam also consciously used the same networks for the spreading of their faiths. As the cultural, economic, and technological arteries that linked empires, kingdoms, and trade communities over many centuries – including those of the Chinese, Sogdians, Sassanians, Byzantines, Mongols, Turks, and Genovese among many, many others – the Eurasian networks facilitated interactions among people from diverse cultures and promoted an unprecedented sharing of commodities, ideas, arts, sciences, belief systems, and innovations.

This interaction of people from diverse cultures also enabled musical contacts in ways that were as varied as they were complex. Together with silk, borax, yak tails, peacock feathers, jasmine, saffron, and lapis lazuli, musical instruments had been moving across the caravan trails of Eurasia since very early times. We know, for example, that ensembles characteristic of various locales outside Chinese cultural spheres – Central Asia, the Tarim Basin, Korea, etc. – introduced different "exotic" musical flavors to imperial festivities at the Chinese court from as early as the Northern Wei dynasty (386–534) to as late as the Qing dynasty (1644–1912). Musicians and their instruments were willingly or forcibly moved around and sometimes settled in far-off lands, often at the invitation or command of an eager new patron or in the aftermath of war and conquest. After the fall of Baghdad to the Mongols in 1258, for example, the last ʿAbbasid caliph's famous music theorist and master musician-singer Ṣafī al-Dīn al-Urmawī (1216–94) so impressed Hülegü Khan (r. 1256–65) with his art, skill, and erudition that he found gainful employment at the Mongol court. And in the fourteenth century, the Moroccan traveler Ibn Battuta reported that during his sojourn in al-Kansa (Hangzhou), he attended a banquet hosted by the Yuan city administrator at which "[t]he amir's son sailed in another [ship] with musicians and singers who sang in Chinese, Arabic and Persian," over the course of a program including a song with a wonderful tune on a text by the Persian poet Saadi Shirazi (1210–91/92) (Ibn Battuta 1994: 903). Many other such documented instances of cultural intersections reveal the folly of exclusively studying premodern Eurasian musical cultures from the perspective of contacts between static and bounded regional cultures.

Cosmopolitan musical practices and instruments were by no means unique to the powerful capitals of Tang Chang'an, Yuan Hangzhou, 'Abbasid Baghdad, or Timurid Herat. In the aftermath of frequent cultural encounters in the Eurasian expanses, it sometimes happened that musical objects originally characteristic to a specific area were adopted by various other groups, each of which may have altered not only the associated social and performative practices but also the meanings and music traditions proper with which these instruments were associated elsewhere. In other cases, musical instruments and practices remained strongly, though seldom exclusively, associated with the organological world of a particular ethnolinguistic group, and their historical patterns of circulation mapped onto the movements, expansions, and contractions of that group across large swaths of Eurasian lands.

Musical instruments, their surrounding practices, and their Eurasian stories are at the heart of this Element. The mechanisms that favored their individual Eurasian journeys, and their adoption, adaptation, or rejection by various cultures, are as diverse as they are intricate. They were, in part at least, contingent upon the intensity of the initial cultural encounter and the power relations between the two participating cultural realms, as well as the systems of patronage and intracultural social dynamics and aesthetics involved. It is important to note that musical instruments, as material objects, circulated along Eurasian trade routes and beyond more easily than wholesale music repertoires or dances since, as a rule, instruments are easily reproducible and thus culturally more adaptable. Portability and intrinsic physical features such as frets and tone holes, for example, reflect and transmit fundamental music conceptions of intonation, pitch, and scale, yet these are often the artefactual characteristics most readily modified, adapted, or removed to suit local practices. As ethnomusicologists have long acknowledged, however, beyond their physicality musical instruments "are embedded within the systems of thought that organize and give coherence to a particular world view" (Becker 1988: 385). To the informed and receptive listener, as Megan Rancier reminds us, "the musical instrument functions simultaneously as a reminder of where the instrument came from, the people who have played it, contexts in which it has been played, and emotional associations with the instrument and its contexts" (Rancier 2014: 381). However, among members of its new adoptive community, any musical instrument may ultimately retain or lose parts or even all of the superstructural complex of meanings, values, and associations it once evoked. This intersection of materiality, morphology, and cultural meaning creates the fascinating stories of each musical instrument in the Eurasian world.

Information pertaining to music-related objects or practices and their transcultural journeys comes from diverse sources, and its interpretation requires approaches informed by methodologies from a wide array of scholarly fields: archaeology, historical linguistics, textual and visual studies, anthropology, and ethnomusicology, among others. For example, from visual representations in manuscripts, murals, and carvings, one can carefully determine aspects of the morphology of musical instruments, details regarding ensembles, particulars of dance movements and choreographies, as well as performance contexts and even cultural meanings. Texts of a wide variety of types, including religious and literary writings, travel literature, and diplomatic documents, offer a different type of information, in which the names of instruments or musical practices may be given; the aural world that they engender may be described and, at times, judged; and comparative aesthetic hierarchies may be established. Insofar as musical objects are concerned, actual instruments from the premodern era – such as the Gogen Biwa in the Shōsōin – have survived only in rare and remarkable cases. Most have been found by archaeologists – often in fragmentary state – in burials, thereby attesting to their status in their respective cultures, and thus to the fact that they had been sufficiently valued to be interred in the company of corpses, weapons, and treasure hoards.

The extant evidence – be that iconographic, textual and linguistic, or archaeological – is unevenly distributed across the vastness of Eurasia and disproportionally favors one or another culture in different ways. This can be due to the vicissitudes of history and geography (e.g. wars, destruction in the aftermath of conquest, desertification, melting of the permafrost, levels of ground humidity, etc.), to the kind of materials used for the construction of the instrument or of the media of their visualization or description (e.g. types of wood, paper, ceramic, metal, birch bark, etc.), or to systems of patronage or sociocultural habits that varyingly privileged the visual, textual, oral, or aural. These stories, then, are never complete and final, and new evidence of an unexpected nature may lurk around the corner that provides new complexity and enriches our understanding. But they are not unrecoverable.

In an attempt to make sense of the bewildering diversity of issues that characterize the study of music in premodern Eurasia, this Element offers five stories that sketch historical and geographical trajectories of music-related objects, practices, or sound-making devices, as articulated in the aftermath of music-cultural encounters and associated entanglements. On the one hand, our stories start from the premise that the spread of musical instruments and practices in early Eurasia took place both through "long-distance" transmission and as a result of networking "contact expansion" (Zürcher 1990: 158–82). On the other hand, they build to a large extent upon the work of scholars such as La Vaissière (2005) and Whitfield (2019), who sought to shift the conversation away from the east–west axis of transmission and interaction, and to highlight the presence of interregional hubs where north–south encounters played at least as important a role.

The stories featured here range from the geographically diverse performing groups and the most famous "foreign" dances during the Tang era, to the elusive musical world of Kucha in the Tarim Basin – a veritable nexus in the network of trans-Eurasian musical commerce. They also recount the fragmentary history of a single instrument linked to the movement of the Turkic peoples across Eurasia, and the circulation of a technological trope – the sound-making automata including the organ – on both east–west and north–south axes. Ultimately, they are but five compelling tales among the many others that await their telling.

2 The Cosmopolitan Chang'an

2.1 Introduction

In the eighth century, Chang'an was among the most cosmopolitan cities in the world. It housed tens of thousands of foreign residents hailing from virtually every country in Asia. No doubt the convergence of the musical practices of all these communities yielded a lively and diverse urban soundscape, but more remarkable than the exotic sounds these foreign residents provided was the already cosmopolitan musical mix celebrated at the center of power, the imperial court.

The scale of the human forces involved in the court music and dance ensembles of the Tang was astonishing. At its peak under Emperor Xuanzong 玄宗 (r. 712–56), the total is said to have run to some 30,000 musicians and dancers in various capacities (Schafer 1963: 52). The forces even extended to the non-human: Xuanzong was partial to trained horses, and kept hundreds that were trained to dance (Thilo 2006: 501). In part these numbers were due to the large number of divisions within the musical bureaucracy, each of which maintained separate membership. There were four court institutions, the Grand Music Bureau (*Dayue shu* 大樂署), the Drum and Wind Music Bureau (*Guchui shu* 鼓吹署), the Entertainment Bureau (*Jiaofang* 教坊), and the Pear Garden

(*Liyuan* 梨園). Within each of these were multiple subgroups with different functions, each of which could perform independently.

The kind of performance most associated with the Tang is the spectacles known as *yanyue* 燕樂, literally "banquet music." The name derived from its typical performance occasion as entertainment during a banquet. The term *yanyue* is not to be confused with the more formal *yayue* ("elegant music"). The latter term designated the more refined and prestigious forms of ceremonial music that were extolled in the Chinese classics in the first millennium BCE. *Yanyue* was also an ancient term and practice, but it had always been overshadowed by *yayue* in the discourse. However, by the Tang, though *yayue* continued to serve the important legitimizing function as part of the state sacrifices, it drew much less attention than the courtly entertainment music. Some of the foreigners may have even misunderstood the distinction between the two; for instance, the Japanese applied the term *yayue* (using kanji which they pronounced *gagaku*) for musical practices that clearly derived from *yanyue*. Indeed, foreign emissaries were far more likely to be shown the splendor of the entertainment music, which would flaunt the court's enviable resources, than the power of the ritual music, which could potentially be harnessed against them (Picken 1985b: 8 and 1987: 46).

However, it is important to note that these distinctions were never as clear as the typology suggests. *Yayue* had traditionally been opposed to *suyue* 俗樂 ("popular music"), which represented popular songs useful for entertainment but not for ritual, and *huyue* 胡樂 ("barbarian music"), which was for outsiders. But by the mid-Tang, this three-way distinction no longer clearly applied. Popular music increasingly drew upon foreign elements, and developed into what was called "new popular music" (*xin suyue* 新俗樂), which served as banquet music. But this new banquet music also served important ritual functions that came to mimic the state sacrifices in various ways, and was even designated as "new elegant music" (*xin yayue* 新雅樂) (Gimm 1966: 135).

However, despite the conspicuous presence of foreign elements, there were ways in which the cosmopolitanism of Tang musical performances was not a wholesale adoption of foreign cultural ideas, but rather a superficial veneer that reinforced a number of longstanding aspects of Chinese music ideology. First, the domain of music should not be understood as limited to the sound of vocal and instrumental music, but was much larger, including at least costume and dance, and at times what we might categorize as even less musical forms like acrobatics. The *Record of Music* (*Yueji* 樂記, c. 300 BCE) treats music as part of a continuum of increasing expressiveness of interior states: "Poetry expresses intention, song extends the sounds, and dance moves the countenance; these three are based in the heart" (詩言其志也, 歌詠其聲也, 舞動其容也, 三者本於心)

(ctext 19.33[2]). Elsewhere it clarifies that the addition of feathers and axes (implying dance props and costumes) yields the most fully realized and cultured form of music, that which separates "music" (*yue* 樂) from mere "tones" (*yin* 音) (Cook 1995: 19–22, 25–27). These visual elements were also essential to the Sui and Tang cosmopolitan forms, which were used as grandiose entertainment.

Second, music was bureaucratized, with musical agents distributed into various departments with different functions. This is a musical version of the vision of government in the *Rites of Zhou* (*Zhou Li* 周禮, c. third century BCE), which purports to describe the governing institutions of the Western Zhou period (c. 1045–771 BCE), a period revered as a golden age by Confucius and his followers. Among the institutions whose members and duties are enumerated in the *Rites of Zhou* are several kinds of music directors, musicians, and craftspeople. As noted, official music functions in the Tang were divided into four separate divisions, but within each of these were suborganizations with a fully bureaucratic structure, all in a scheme of vastly larger proportions than its classical predecessors.

Third, music was typically organized using geographic designations in ways that emulate the pattern set by the *Classic of Poetry* (*Shijing* 詩經, eleventh to seventh centuries BCE). The largest section of the *Classic of Poetry*, the *Airs of the States* (*Guofeng* 國風), is arranged into fifteen sections named after various states within the ancient Chinese ecumene, each of which includes a dozen or so songs that allegedly originated there. The musical content of the songs has been lost, so later scholars often treat them as poems, but we know from accounts elsewhere in the classics that they were sung. Indeed, the *Zuo Commentary to the Spring and Autumn Annals* (*Zuozhuan* 左傳, c. 400 BCE) gives an account of a concert of the *Airs of the States* given to an emissary during an official visit in 543 BCE (DeWoskin 1982: 21–25). This geographical classification of musical materials and its use in diplomacy has echoes in Tang approaches to music.

Finally, in ancient times, sung poetry was recognized as a particularly potent way of expressing oneself, as noted in the passage from the *Record of Music* that included the crystalized phrase *shi yan zhi* (詩言志), meaning "poetry expresses intention." This phrase is even older; its *locus classicus* is in a passage discussing the duties of the Director of Music in the *Classic of Documents* (*Shangshu* 書經). From this ideology, it follows that the authentic folk songs of an area could encode something about the state of the society there, thus music collections could be considered a political tool for conceptualizing and understanding the realm. The fate of societies could also be predicted from the nature of their music. When the music of Zheng 鄭 was played to the emissary in the concert

---

[2] Chinese Text Project: https://ctext.org/liji/yue-ji#n10140.

mentioned in the last paragraph, he predicted based on its extravagant music that it would be the first state to vanish; a century later it did succumb. The music of Zheng and another troubled state Wei 衛 became a metaphor for dangerous music that showed symptoms of social malaise. Though Zheng and Wei proper were located in the Chinese heartland, connecting them with the foreign and thereby suspect was a longstanding trope. Moralists who remembered these lessons looked at faddish music in court with a suspicious eye, worried for what troubles it might foretell.

These four assumptions about the nature of music, that music performance extended beyond sound to spectacle, that it could be bureaucratized, that it could be geographically defined, and that it was politically significant, constituted the frame through which educated Chinese understood music. As they came to encounter music from non-Chinese peoples, it was understood in these terms. During the golden age of Chinese musical cosmopolitanism in Chang'an, foreign musics were everywhere but understood in local terms.

2.2 Bureaucratizing Cosmopolitanism

Following the collapse of the Han dynasty in 220 CE, the Chinese cultural realm entered a prolonged period of disunity that lasted nearly four centuries. When the founder of the Sui dynasty, Emperor Wen 文帝 (r. 581–605), was able to once again consolidate the states, he knew that military conquest alone would not achieve a lasting polity, and thus sought to draw on the legitimizing function of music. During his reign, a series of musical debates took place that involved thirty-seven musicians and theorists from around the realm, including representatives from each of four conquered states: Northern Qi 北齊 (550–77) and Northern Zhou 北周 (557–81) in the north and Liang 梁 (502–87) and Chen 陳 (557–89) in the south (Wang & Sun 2004: 59). The northern territories had been under frequent non-Chinese rule, as Tuoba 拓拔, Tibetan, Xiongnu 匈奴, and Xianbei 鮮卑 tribes fought over the numerous ephemeral states. In the south the regimes had been more stable, but there were many musicians who had fled warring regions or sought opportunities in the southern courts. The participants of the conference thus represented generations of hereditary and master–disciple traditions that had migrated following the vagaries of patronage during rather chaotic centuries (Wang & Sun 2004: 60).

In this way, the Sui emperor attempted to unify musics that represented several distinct traditions. Many of these, particularly in the south, drew upon traditions that continued practices from the Han dynasty and earlier. But others, particularly in the north, brought in practices originating from other communities, often with ties to Central Asia. Moreover, music was often expanded with conquest or hegemonic statecraft; it was "obtained" (*de* 得) as tribute or booty, a terminology that denotes not just the possession of intangible music (which was regarded as real property), but the very tangible instruments, costumes, and performers themselves (Schafer 1963: 51), who entered a status of servitude from which few could leave (Kishibe 1960: 20).

In order to consolidate the disparate musics, the Sui emperor established a musical bureaucracy that divided the banquet music performers into separate units. Each performing division had its own separate personnel (instrumentalists, singers, and dancers), instruments, and costumes. Each group had seven to twenty-five musicians and two to five dancers, except for the larger Banquet Music group, which numbered thirty-one musicians and twenty dancers (Thilo 2006: 492). Initially Emperor Wen established this arrangement as the Seven Performing Divisions (*Qibu yue* 七部樂). The subsequent emperor Yang 煬帝 (r. 604–18) made some modifications and added a few additional divisions, yielding nine; after the Tang conquest of the Sui in 618, this structure continued with minor modifications for a decade before a final overhaul brought the total number to ten. The names of the divisions used in each of these formulations are summarized in Table 1.

Note that each formulation of the system employed geographic names for all but two divisions. Since the number of divisions grew longer as the system was revised, a higher fraction of the performing divisions came to supposedly represent these exotic forms. Despite the foreignizing nomenclature, however, most of these kinds of music were not new to China, having been first attested in Chinese sources in the fourth or fifth century (Yang 1985: 26). Thus, by the time of the Sui, they had had centuries to become familiar and adapt to domestic musical paradigms. In addition to those in a formal group, there were also performers representing Baekje 百濟 and Silla 新羅 (the other two kingdoms in Korea at this time), Göktürks 突厥 (*Tujue*), and Japan (倭國 *Waguo*) (Courant 1913: 192, citing the *Book of Sui* [ctext 15.122[3]]).

According to the *Book of Sui* (*Suishu* 隋書, compiled in 636) and compendium *Tongdian* 通典 ("Comprehensive Institutions," written 766–801), the Seven, Nine, or Ten Performing Divisions would perform together sequentially at large banquets. The resulting suite would go through each of the performing divisions in order. Most of these performances would consist of songs and dances (Sun 2012: 63–64). The serialized performance of the geography echoes the musical tour of the *Classic of Poetry* that seems to have been used diplomatically in the Warring States period.

---

[3] Chinese Text Project: https://ctext.org/wiki.pl?if=gb&chapter=124338.

Table 1 Contents of the Seven, Nine, and Ten Performing Divisions of Sui and Tang court music (after Yang 1985: 26)

QIBU YUE 七部樂 (581)	JIUBU YUE 九部樂 (605)	SHIBU YUE 十部樂 (642)	LITERAL MEANING (PRESENT-DAY LOCATION)
1. Qingshang ji 清商伎	1. Qing ji 清伎	1. Yanyue ji 讌樂伎	Banquet music
		2. Qingshang ji 清商伎	unclear
2. Guo ji 國伎	2. Xiliang ji 西涼伎	3. Xiliang ji 西涼伎	(not geographic, representing a style of Chinese music) "Country," renamed to Liangzhou (Gansu)
		4. Gaochang ji 高昌伎	Turpan (Xinjiang)
3. Qiuci ji 龜茲伎	3. Qiuci ji 龜茲伎	5. Qiuci ji 龜茲伎	Kucha (Xinjiang)
	4. Shule ji 疏勒伎	6. Shule ji 疏勒伎	Kashgar (Xinjiang)
	5. Kangguo ji 康國伎	7. Kangguo ji 康國伎	Samarkand (Uzbekistan)
4. Anguo ji 安國伎	6. Anguo ji 安國伎	8. Anguo ji 安國伎	Bukhara (Uzbekistan)
5. Tianzhu ji 天竺伎	7. Tianzhu ji 天竺伎		India
		9. Funan ji 扶南伎	Funan (Southeast Asia)
6. Gaoli ji 高麗伎	8. Gaoli ji 高麗伎	10. Gaoli ji 高麗伎	Goguryeo (Korea)
7. Wenkang ji 文康伎			"Culture and well-being" (representing a masked dance)
	9. Libi ji 禮畢伎		Closing ritual

The full name of each performing division can use ji 伎 ("technique") and yue 樂 ("music") interchangeably.

Emperor Xuanzong in the mid-Tang reorganized the musical system, so that music was no longer divided along geographical or ethnic lines, but into two types (*erbuji* 二部伎), the functional categories "standing music" (*libuji* 立部伎) and "sitting music" (*zuobuji* 座部伎) (Yang 1985: 27). The former was performed mainly outdoors by larger groups of standing performers, while the latter was performed by smaller seated groups as a chamber ensemble. The repertoire of each of the two types was much more rigidly fixed than the earlier categorization; rather than indicating geographically named ensembles and styles, the formulation called for eight specific standing pieces and six specific sitting pieces. However, the performances could be more selective within this repertoire, instead of following the set sequence of performing divisions as a suite. These changes did not erase the musical ensembles of the earlier Tang, but simply reorganized them in an increasingly rigid and deterritorialized way. Some have argued that this bureaucratic change reflected the increased Sinicization of previously imported styles (Liang 1985: 99). Other writers refer instead to a "fusion" between Chinese and foreign musics (Sun 2012: 65). Indeed, it may be more appropriate to call it an increased Kucheanization, as the majority of the accompanying ensembles drew heavily on Kuchean music, whatever style of music they purported to represent (Yang 1985: 27).

A more unambiguous Sinicization occurred in 754, when Xuanzong ordered the official renaming of fifty-eight pieces of non-Chinese origin, most often altering the titles from transliterations of other languages to translations into Chinese; all 215 items in the repertory were inscribed in stone, using their new titles if modified (Yang 1985: 28). Though there is no indication that the pieces themselves were modified, they were marked as Chinese instead of having an obvious foreign origin, and once again the extent of the repertory became more rigid, as they were literally written in stone. Not long after this change, political chaos forced the gradual abandonment of this system, and by the end of the Tang in the early tenth century foreign music was treated and thought of rather differently.

2.3 Foreign Musics and Instruments

Most of the information we know about the performing divisions comes from lists of instruments that they incorporated. The list of instruments in the nine performing divisions of the late Sui dynasty are summarized in Table 2; following modern organological convention, the instruments are divided into four categories according to their sound-making element. A glance at the table makes it immediately clear that the ensembles would have rather distinctive

Table 2 Instrumentation in the Nine Performing Divisions of the Late Sui, as indicated in the *Book of Sui* (ctext 15.124–136;[4] see also Courant 1913: 192–94).

PERFORMING DIVISION	IDIOPHONES	CHORDOPHONES	AEROPHONES	MEMBRANOPHONES
QINGSHANG 清商 Chinese Twenty-five players Fifteen instruments	2: Bells (*zhong* 鐘), stone chimes (*qing* 磬)	7: five kinds of zither (*qin* 琴, *se, se* 瑟, bamboo five-string *qin* (*jiqin* 擊琴), *zhu* 筑, and *zheng* 箏), *pipa* 琵琶, *konghou* 箜篌	5: mouth organ (*sheng* 笙), two types of transverse flute (*di* 笛 and *chi* 箎), vertical flute (*xiao* 簫), ocarina (*xun* 塤)	1: rhythm drum (*jiegu* 節鼓, different from *jiegu* later in this table and discussed in the text)
XILIANG 西涼 Liangzhou Twenty-seven players Nineteen instruments	3: Bells, stone chimes, cymbals (*tongbo* 銅鈸)	6: two kinds of zither (*tanzheng* 彈箏 and *chouzheng* 搊箏), *konghou*, upright harp (*shu konghou* 竪箜篌), four-string *pipa*, five-string *pipa*	7: mouth organ, vertical flute, two sizes of *bili* 篳篥, long flute (*changdi* 長笛), flute (*hengdi* 橫笛), conch (*bei* 貝)	3: waist drum (*yaogu* 腰鼓), *qigu* 齊鼓, shoulder drum (*dangu* 担鼓)

4 Chinese Text Project: https://ctext.org/wiki.pl?if=gb&chapter=124338.

Table 2 (cont.)

Performing division	Idiophones	Chordophones	Aerophones	Membranophones
Qiuci 龜兹 Kucha Twenty players Fifteen instruments	1: cymbals	3: upright harp, four-string *pipa*, five-string *pipa*	5: *sheng*, transverse flute (*di*), vertical flute, *bili*, conch	6: *maoyuangu* 毛員鼓, *dutangu* 都曇鼓, *dalagu* 答腊鼓, *jiegu* 羯鼓, *jilougu* 鸡婁鼓, waist drum
Shule 疏勒 Kashgar Twelve players Ten instruments	0	3: upright harp, four-string *pipa*, five-string *pipa*	3: transverse flute (*di*), vertical flute, *bili*	4: *dalagu*, waist drum, *jiegu*, *jilougu*
Kangguo 康國 Samarkand Seven players Four instruments	2: cymbals, bronze drum	0	1: transverse flute (*di*)	1: *jiagu* 加鼓
Anguo 安國 Bukhara Twelve players Ten instruments	1: cymbals	3: *konghou*, four-string *pipa*, five-string *pipa*	4: transverse flute (*di*), vertical flute, *bili*, double *bili*	2: *zhenggu* 正鼓, *hegu* 和鼓
Tianzhu 天竺 India Twelve players Nine instruments	2: bronze drum (*tonggu* 銅鼓), cymbals	3: phoenix-head harp (*fengshou konghou* 凤首箜篌), four-string *pipa*, five-string *pipa*	2: transverse flute (*di*), conch	2: *maoyuangu*, *dutangu*

GAOLI 高麗 Goguryeo Eighteen players Fourteen instruments	0	5: zither (*tanzheng*), *konghou*, upright harp, four-string *pipa*, five-string *pipa*	6: transverse flute (*di*), mouth organ, vertical flute, small *bili*, peach skin *bili* 桃皮篳篥, conch	3: waist drum, *jigu*, shoulder drum
LIBI 禮畢 Closing ritual Twenty-two players Seven instruments	1: Jingle bells (*lingpan* 鈴盤)	0	4: two kinds of transverse flute (*di* and *chi*), vertical flute, mouth organ	2: waist drum, handle drum (*bing* 鞞)

sound profiles from one another. We know the total number of players and instrumentalists in each group, so can see that many – though not all – of the ensembles were mostly composed of solo performers, and may have relied on coloristic effects of distinctive individual timbres. Some divisions are considerably larger than others. But where they really differ is in the types of instruments that made them up. The group that was perceived as "Chinese" had only one type of drum, while the ensemble from Kucha had six. Some ensembles (like those representing China or Korea) had a large number of plucked string instruments (none of them use bowed strings, which may not have been invented yet), while others (like that representing Kucha) had none. Meanwhile the most prestigious instruments of the ancient Chinese tradition, the chimes of bells (*bianzhong* 編鐘) and stones (*bianqing* 編磬), were only used in those ensembles that were perceived to be part of that tradition (that is, those recognized as "Chinese"). Certain instruments, such as the four-string *pipa* and the transverse flute *di*, could be found in the majority of the ensembles, though there are also several instruments, especially unusual drums, that were specifically associated with only one ensemble.

Two of the earliest "foreign" musics to gain a foothold in China, those representing Kucha and Liangzhou, became some of the most familiar to the Tang court. According to the *Old Book of Tang* (*Jiu Tangshu* 舊唐書, compiled 945), even before the Sui unification in 581, the majority of mixed-ensemble pieces had used Liangzhou music, while drum and dance pieces typically had used Kuchean music (Yang 1985: 27). Due to the prominence of Kuchean and Liangzhou music, they came to influence the other styles as well. This is perhaps fitting, since Kucha and Liangzhou music were heterogeneous to start with and served as conduits for other kinds of music. This sort of lateral influence undercut the tidy classification schemes of the court music from the very beginning and may have contributed to the reorganization and renaming under Xuanzong that obscured geographic origins.

Liangzhou (also referred to as "Xiliang" 西涼, meaning "Western Liang") was located about halfway between the Sui capital Chang'an and Dunhuang in an area with a significant Chinese population. Music from this area was not perceived as wholly foreign but was regarded instead as a mixture of Chinese and local elements deriving from other ethnicities (hence the earlier name *Guoji* 國伎 "country music"). This is clearly visible in the instrumentation, which combines what were universally regarded as traditional Chinese instruments (particularly the bell and stone chimes) with those associated with Kucha (such as various drums, the *bili*, and the five-string *pipa*, known as the Kuchean *pipa*).

Kucha (present-day Kuqa, Aksu Prefecture in Xinjiang) was located in the Tarim Basin, along with the namesake origins of two other bureaucratized styles of music, Turfan and Kashgar. The traveling monk Xuanzang 玄奘 (602–64) already singled out Kucha's musical fame when he passed through it in 630, noting that "their skill in playing wind and stringed instruments is well known in various countries" (Xuanzang 1996: 17). (For the Kucheans' own view on their musicianship, see Section 4.) Certainly, their repertoire as it appeared in the court in Chang'an was much more expansive than that of other territories: in the list of titles of full-ensemble pieces in the compendium *Tongzhi* 通志 ("Comprehensive Records," 1161), the Kuchean division has twenty entries, while most others had only a few; Goguryeo (Korea) and India had only two each (Courant 1913: 192n9).

Xuanzang also noted the extent to which Indian culture had influenced Kucha, particularly in terms of language and religion. It is thus conceivable that the music of Kucha may also have been shaped in part at least by Indian musical traditions (see Section 4). For instance, it is possible the *dalagu* 答腊鼓, a pair of small drums played with the fingers, may be related in form, technique, and even name to the *tabla* which remains common in Indian music today (Gimm 1966: 177–78). At the Chinese court, though, the performing divisions representing India and Kucha remained rather distinct in terms of instrumentation: Kuchean music was associated foremost with prominent winds and drums, while Indian music focused more on strings. Among the strings in the Indian performing division was the phoenix-head harp (*fengshou konghou* 鳳首箜篌), unique among the performing divisions, which (though Courant 1913: 193 assimilates it to the peacock-headed *manyuri* of India) is perhaps connected with the music of Southeast Asia, as it appears in the ensemble sent from Pyu in Burma two centuries later (Twitchett and Christie 1959: 186; on this ensemble, see p. 20).

It is impossible to separate these influences from geopolitics. Histories of music often associate the rise of Kuchean music in China with Lü Guang 呂光 (337–400), a general of the Former Qin 秦 (351–94) who conquered Kucha in 385 and proceeded to establish his own short-lived state, the Later Liang 涼 (386–403; Liang as in Liangzhou, with a capital in that area). Lü Guang himself was ethnically Di 氐, one of the seminomadic groups that established states in northern China in the fourth century; its relationship with other ethnic groups is uncertain, but it may have been Turkic or Tibetan. In fact, the nature of Lü Guang's vaunted connection with Kuchean music is difficult to establish; contemporaneous sources do not discuss music and even later compendia like the *Tongdian* credit him only with "obtaining the music" (*de qi sheng* 得其聲), not promoting or spreading it. According to the *Tongdian*, the music was not passed down after Lü's death in 400, and it was only through reconquest of the region in 439 under the succeeding Later Wei 魏 dynasty (386–535) that the music was transmitted into the Chinese heartland (Gimm 1966: 209).

Within Chang'an, Kucha became renowned for its music, song, and dance, which happened to be the sort of spectacle that played well at Chinese court banquets. This reputation grew especially under the patronage of supportive rulers like Emperor Wenxuan 文宣 of the Northern Qi (r. 550–59), who is said to have played a Kuchean drum himself (known as *hugu* 胡鼓 in the sources, literally "foreign drum," which could denote any of several different instruments) (Gimm 1966: 209). By this time a number of Kuchean musicians resided in Chang'an and passed on their musical traditions there. Perhaps the most famous, Cao Miaoda 曹妙達, whose grandfather Cao Poluomen 曹婆羅門 was among the earliest-known players of the Kuchean *pipa*, was even made a prince by the Sui emperor Wendi 文帝 (Gimm 1966: 210, 374). In fact, many of the best-known musicians that were identified as foreign in historical sources were not foreign-born and had resided in China for generations, though they continued to be considered authentic purveyors of their "exotic" musical traditions (Chou 1976: 233). Indeed, the Cao family achieved the status of a musical dynasty within the Tang, famed for their musical talents, especially but not exclusively on the *pipa* (Picken 1987: 113; Gimm 1966: 374–75; see also, Section 4, p. 38).

The drums of the Kuchean performing division were especially famed, and they had more of them than any other division, although none of them were used by this ensemble alone. One of the most prominent was the drum *jiegu* 羯鼓, which was popular among the nobility, including Emperor Xuanzong himself, who studied it (Schafer 1963: 52). The drum had a cylindrical or hourglass shape, with heads on both sides, played using sticks by a seated performer (Gimm 1966: 458–59). The instrument may ultimately be of Indian origin (459), though the name suggests a connection with the Jie 羯 people, a tribe that thrived in northern China in the fourth century and may be related to the present-day Ket, an Indigenous people of Siberia whose language is unrelated to other extant groups (Vovin et al. 2016). However, the word *jie* may also be taken at face value with its native meaning of "castrated ram," leading to the Schafer's translation as "wether drum" (Schafer 1963: 52). The *jiegu* seems to have been quite popular, since it was included in the Indian, Kashgar, Kucha, and Turfan ensembles (Gimm 1966: 459).

The wind instrument most associated with Kucha was the *bili* 篳篥, a piercing double-reed instrument similar to the oboe, generally with seven holes on top and two underneath. The *Tongdian* evocatively says of this instrument that its "original name is the 'bamboo of sadness.' It came from among the barbarians (*hu*); its voice is sorrowful" (本名悲篥, 出於胡中, 其聲悲; ctext 144.8.8[5]). Though it was specifically associated with Kucha, it was also used in the ensembles from Liangzhou, Bukhara, Turfan, Korea, India, and Kashgar, that is, the majority of the performing divisions (Gimm 1966: 437). Though its Kuchean identity remained strong, it was also used in military ensembles in the Tang as well, even though they were technically classified as *yayue* (439). That the *bili* came in a variety of sizes and styles can be ascertained from Table 2; the Bukhara ensemble used a double *bili* that may be somehow connected with the double pipes of much farther west in ancient times. The instrument survives in Chinese music today, usually now called the *guan* 管, and is also the ancestor of the prominent *gagaku* instrument *hichiriki* whose name derives from *bili* and is written with the same characters.

One string instrument that was also highly associated with Kucha was the five-string *pipa*, known in Chinese sources under various names, among which the most common is *wuxian pipa* 五弦琵琶 (literally "five-string *pipa*"), itself a type of lute that might have entered Kucha from India (see also Section 4, p. 43). Other names include the *hu-pipa* (the 'barbarian' [Western Regions] *pipa*) and the *Qiuci-pipa* (Kuchean *pipa*) (Myers 1992: 8). The five-string, straight-neck *pipa* should be distinguished from the four-string *pipa* that had been used in China earlier, and had gained greater acceptance to the extent that it was included in the Qingyue performing division, which represented "pure" Chinese music. The Kuchean *pipa* was probably introduced to China during the Northern Wei (386–535) and became popular after about 500 (Gimm 1966: 316).

As can be seen in Table 1, most of the regions represented in the Ten Performing Divisions were in Central Asia. The Tang, at its greatest extent, included several of those named, though there were also others further west, such as Samarkand and Bukhara in the area of Sogdiana (present-day Uzbekistan), which were never part of the Tang Empire per se. When the Umayyad and Abbasid Caliphates expanded into these regions in the eighth century, they interacted less frequently with the Tang, and the presence of Sogdian musical culture in China weakened. Meanwhile, however, the regions to the south of the Tang became increasingly incorporated into the system. In the final recension of the performing divisions in 642, for example, Indian music was replaced with music from Funan 扶南, located in Southeast Asia. Our knowledge about the Funan state (or states) is quite uncertain, since it is known primarily through Chinese sources. Like a mirror of Kucha, though, it seems to have had significant Indian influence in terms of religion and script, and likely

---

[5] Chinese Text Project: https://ctext.org/text.pl?node=560420&if=en#n560428.

music as well. Indeed, previously, the two dancers that were part of the Indian performing division in fact hailed from Funan (Courant 1913: 193).

Later, other states based in present-day southwestern China and Burma also came into the picture. According to the *New Tang History*, in 794, King Yimouxun 異牟尋 of Nanzhao 南詔 (r. 779–808) sent an embassy to the Tang court, including a request to offer a troupe of singers and dancers as tribute, as part of a diplomatic mission seeking allies against the expanding Tibetan Empire. From the Nanzhao troupe, the receiving military governor (*jiedushi* 節度使) in Chengdu, Wei Gao 韋皋 (745–805), put together a cycle of music using the musicians and sixty-four dancers, which became part of the permanent repertoire. The Nanzhao emissary also brought the message that the more distant Pyu states (called *Piao* 驃 in the Chinese sources) also wished to send a troupe with them. The Pyu states sent a delegation in 802, including thirty-five musicians, twenty-two instruments, and a dozen pieces of music (Twitchett & Christie 1959: 177 and 185). As arranged by Wei Gao, the performances came to resemble *yayue* in their use of feathers in rigid square arrangements of dancers, a few highly indexical instruments (the "thunder drum" *leigu* 雷鼓 and bells), a modal structure drawing on classical Chinese theory, and offerings of homage, all highly suggestive of a surrender ritual (Gimm 1966: 231–32). In this way Southeast Asian music also came to be incorporated within the Tang musical system, though it was much less influential than so-called Western music.

While China was a recipient of numerous musical traditions, it also served as a conduit to other places. Whenever foreign delegations visited the court, the spectacular performances could hardly have failed to make an impression. But it was Japan in particular that became especially interested in reproducing similar performances at home. When the scholar Kibi no Makibi 吉備真備 (695–775) returned to Japan after having studied in Chang'an for seventeen years, among his many personal effects were tuning pipes, instruments (including the Gogen Biwa), compositions, and a compendium of musical matters, the *Records of the Essentials in the Book of Music* (樂書要錄, Ch. *Yueshu yaolu*, Jp. *Gakusho yoroku*) (Garfias 1975: 9). While there were many missions from Japan to Tang China for purposes of statecraft and politics, several, including those of 630, 653, 701, 717, and 751, focused on culture (Picken & Nickson 1997: 2). There were also performances of Chinese musicians in Japan, a practice that the Tang government encouraged. In 766, the officials Huangfu Dongchao 皇甫東朝 and Huangfu Shengnü 皇甫昇女 received promotions after they performed Tang court music in a Buddhist temple in Nara (Wang 2005: 204). The last Japanese mission to the Tang was in 838–41 and included the musician Fujiwara no Sadatoshi (藤原貞敏, 807–67), who studied *pipa* in Yangzhou and Chang'an and married his teacher's daughter. He returned to Japan with scores of banquet music and went on to become head of the Bureau of Music and Dancing in 847 (Wang 2005: 307, n. 30). As a result of these cultural interchanges, Tang court music came to be replicated in Japan as *gagaku*.

2.4 Genres and Repertoire

The most important genre of banquet music in the Sui and Tang eras was the three-part suite known as the *daqu* 大曲, "great suite." The three parts are not to be identified with movements; instead, each was itself composed of many discrete pieces. Generally, the opening part (*sanxu* 散序 "free prelude") was a suite of instrumental unmetered melodies that progressed through different modes and different instruments, concluding with a transition to a metrical structure. The middle part (*zhongxu* 中序 "middle prelude") centered around the accompanied voice, may or may not have included dance elements, and was generally slow but transitioned to a moderate pace toward the end. The final section (*po* 破 "breakdown") focused on dance, and progressed through a series of conventionally named subsections, gradually accelerating to a dizzying tempo before coming back down in the final subsections. While these sections were typical, there was considerable variety in the formal structure of actual pieces (Yang 1985: 32). The *daqu* form developed from earlier Chinese models such as the *Xianghe ge* 相和歌 ("Harmonious song") of the Han dynasty (Sun 2012: 38). However, by the Tang it was typical for *daqu* to incorporate foreign elements.

When the Japanese modeled their music after the Tang, they adopted this formal tripartite structure, but modified it into *jo-ha-kyū* 序破急 ("introduction, breakdown, and rushing") (Picken 1985b: 97). These terms do not derive directly from the nomenclature of the three parts of *daqu*, but rather the opening two parts (which were both labelled *xu* 序 "prelude"), the opening of the third part, and the climax. The *jo-ha-kyū* structure, which was initially applied to form in *gagaku*, had what is surely one of the most remarkable afterlives of Eurasian musical exchanges. It was centuries later adopted by Zeami Motokiyo 世阿弥 元清 (c. 1363–c. 1443), one of the principal developers of Noh 能 theater, as a description of movement in general. From there it went on to become a general aesthetic principle that is used in arts as diverse as theater, martial arts, tea ceremony, and poetry.

Probably the best-known of the *daqu* was "The Qin Prince Breaks the Enemy Ranks" (*Qin wang po zhen yue* 秦王破陣樂), later also known as "Dance of Seven Virtues" (*Qi de wu* 七德舞). It commemorated the early Tang military victory of 620, when the then-Prince of Qin Li Shimin 李世民, the younger brother of the founding emperor, defeated a rebelling commander and thereby solidified the new dynasty. According to the account in the *Tang Huiyao* 唐會要

("Institutional History of the Tang"), the people commemorated the victory in a song (Gimm 1966: 215). After Li Shimin succeeded his brother to become the second Tang emperor Taizong 太宗 (r. 626–49), he commissioned a lyricist and a composer to arrange this folk song into a *daqu*. Choreographies of the piece were of enormous scale; according to the *Old Book of Tang* it featured 120 dancers clad in armor and various military props. On special occasions, such as banquets for returning armies, it could even be larger, with some 2,000 participants and an army of horses (Sun 2012: 68–69).

The piece was classified within the Kuchean division (Gimm 1966: 207), so it not surprisingly featured prominent percussion, including the conspicuous role of the thunder drum (*leidagu* 雷大鼓) played with such vigor that it was said to have shaken everything within 100 miles (Thilo 2006: 494). The song was immensely popular; after Xuanzong's reorganization it was included in both the sitting music and standing music, with the sitting music using a shortened version (Wang & Sun 2004: 52). The piece continued to be performed in Chang'an throughout the Tang dynasty (Thilo 2006: 494), but it also traveled widely. When the Buddhist pilgrim Xuanzang met King Bhaskarvarman of Kumarupa (in present-day Northeast India) in about 640, the king claimed that the song was chanted among the people of many Indian states (Xuanzang 1996: 265–66). While this seems unlikely, the role that the song plays in this diplomatic episode illustrates that it must have achieved a huge fame quickly and that Xuanzang's Chinese readership must have considered it to have great cultural prestige. More plausibly, in the early ninth century the Tang envoy Liu Yuanding 刘元鼎 reports seeing a performance of it in Turfan, which by then was no longer part of the Tang realm (Kapstein 2009: 28–29). Notation for a piece with a similar name (*Ō-dai hajin-raku* 皇帝破陣樂, "The Emperor Breaks the Enemy Ranks") survives in several independent Japanese sources, the earliest from 1171 (Picken 1985a: 72); while these may represent only an imitation of that kind of music made at the Heian court (see the arguments summarized in Liang 1984: 360–61), the fact that this title was chosen for such a piece is telling of its prestige abroad.

Faqu 法曲 was an important subtype of *daqu*. The meaning of the name is unclear. *Fa* 法 can mean "order" or "rule," perhaps implying that it conformed to a particular pattern. But *fa* also denotes a kind of Daoist magic. The existence of several pieces in the genre with Daoist associations suggests that may be the intended meaning, so perhaps something like "magical pieces" is closer to the original signification (Picken 1985a: 47). It may even be connected with the Buddhist concept of dharma, which was rendered as *fa* in Chinese translations. *Faqu* was distinguished by the ensemble used, which was closer to *qingyue* (the performing divisions that represented Chinese music), and was thus more subdued than the Kuchean-influenced ensembles (Yang 1985: 32). *Faqu* was the special purview of the performers in the Pear Garden (Yang 1985: 46), the music department established by Emperor Xuanzong and directly under his personal leadership.

Undoubtedly the best-known of the *faqu* was "Music of Rainbow Skirts and Feather Robes" (霓裳羽衣曲 *Nichang yuyi qu*). It had thirty-six sections, fitting into the standard tripartite form of eighteen instrumental sections, six songs, and twelve dance pieces (Yang 1985: 33). It is said to have been composed by Emperor Xuanzong, reportedly inspired by a fantastic journey to the moon palace he experienced. Halfway through composing it, he heard the Liangzhou orchestra performing the Indian piece "Poluomen" 婆羅門 and realized that it fit with his suite, and incorporated it (Yang 1985: 34). "Poluomen" is a transliteration of "Brahmin," and the name seems to derive from Buddhist chant practice that was widespread in Central Asia at the time (Gimm 1966: 294–96). How the chant might relate to the seemingly instrumental showpiece is unclear, but its incantatory power seems quite appropriate for a *faqu*. The "Music of Rainbow Skirts and Feather Robes" remained popular into the ninth century; the poet Bai Juyi 白居易 (772–846) saw a performance of it at court in 808–9, and later tried to recreate it as governor of Hangzhou and Suzhou (Waley 1949: 154); he wrote a poem about it in 825.

2.5 The Moralistic Backlash

Despite the fame at home and abroad the spectacles of the Tang court achieved, it was often accompanied by an ambivalence that the music had deviated too far from classical norms of music. During the first century and a half of the Tang, such complaints were muted by the obvious vigor of the state; it was hard to argue morality when a string of military victories seemed to confirm its possession of the Mandate of Heaven. However, after the An Lushan Rebellion (755–63), it became much less clear that Heaven favored the court, and critics came forward to voice the opinion that the chaos was the inevitable result of a court that welcomed unorthodox music and allowed it to outweigh the proper ritual music, just as had supposedly happened in ancient times in the states of Zheng and Wei.

Among the most strident critics was the minister and poet Yuan Zhen 元稹 (779–831), the more conservative friend of Bai Juyi. In Yuan's poem "The Stone Chimes of Huayuan" (*Huayuan qing* 华原磬), he uses the ancient musical instrument of stone chimes as a symbol of how the fad for the new had usurped the role of orthodox music. Instead of using the traditional stone for the instrument, Xuanzong had ordered the chimes to adopt exotic stones that pleased his favorite concubine Yang Guifei 楊貴妃 (719–56), who performed on them (Schafer 1963: 287, n. 230). Thereby the court abandoned the musical principles prescribed in the classics like "Yellow Bell" (*huangzhong* 黃鐘, the designation for the correct standard pitch) and "Cloud Gate" (*Yunmen* 雲門, an ancient dance performed in ritual). Following the trope, the blame is partially placed on petty officials who embrace the fads, but Yuan goes so far as to blame Xuanzong himself for the neglect of the proper music:

華原軟石易追琢，	The soft stone of Huayuan is substituted for the polished,
高下隨人無雅鄭。	From high to low the followers ignore the elegant and corrupt.
棄舊美新由樂胥，	The petty music officials discard the old and decorate the new;
自此黃鐘不能競。	From this the Yellow Bell cannot compete.
玄宗愛樂愛新樂，	Xuanzong loves music, he loves the new music,
梨園弟子承恩橫。	The pupils in the Pear Garden carry forth the perversion he has bestowed.
霓裳才徹胡騎來，	"Rainbow Skirts" then penetrates and the barbarians ride in on horses,
雲門未得蒙親定。	"Cloud Gate" has not yet been able to pacify the uncultured clans.

(Chinese text from ctext[6])

The concern for preserving the classical past is in part defending it against innovations from outside that usurped the orthodox, but this is often combined with more than a little bit of racism against those outsiders. His poem *Faqu* 法曲, named after the genre, illustrates this racial resentment particularly clearly:

自從胡騎起煙塵，	Ever since barbarian cavalry raised smoke and dust,
毛毳腥膻滿咸洛。	The sheep-and-goat stench of felt and furs has filled Chang'an and Luoyang.
女為胡婦學胡妝，	Our women became barbarian wives, learned barbarian makeup;
伎進胡音務胡樂。	Singsong girls offered barbarian tunes, applied themselves to barbarian music.
火鳳聲沉多咽絕，	The tune "The Fire-Roc" was stilled, with much sobbing cut off;

---

[6] Chinese Text Project: https://ctext.org/text.pl?node=187246&if=en.

(cont.)

春鶯囀罷長蕭索。	"The Singing of Spring Warblers" ceased and lapsed forever into silence.
胡音胡騎與胡妝,	Barbarian tunes, barbarian riders, together with barbarian makeup,
五十年來競紛泊。	For fifty years these contended in spreading through [our society].

(Chinese from ctext[7]; tr. Picken 1985a: 48)

The trope of wasted cultural heritage is typical for Yuan, but there is an irony in this poem, for his stand-in piece for the lapsed Confucian orthodoxy, "The Singing of Spring Warblers" (*Chunying Zhuan* 春鶯轉), was written by a Chang'an-born musician of Kuchean descent, Bai Mingda 白明達 (Picken 1985a: 47). Bai Mingda was Rectifier of Music (*yuezheng* 樂正) under Emperor Yangdi 煬帝 of Sui (r. 604–18), possibly having worked in the Later Zhou and Northern Qi courts preceding the Sui. He continued serving in the Tang, at least through mid-century, when this piece is said to have been written (46). Ordinarily in Yuan's poems, a line like this would make a classical allusion (like "Cloud Gate" in the previous poem) to demonstrate what had been lost, so it is already surprising here that he would have chosen something so recent.

Yuan Zhen was not always so uncompromising about popular music and its foreign influences. In his lyric "Song of the Pipa" (*Pipa ge* 琵琶歌), he describes the lively final section ("breakdown" *po* 破, the term designating the third section of the *daqu* form) of a performance on the *pipa*:

月寒一聲深殿磬,	In the cold moonlight, one sound is the chime from deep palace.
驟彈曲破音繁並。	Suddenly playing the breakdown, tunes are busy at once.
百萬金鈴旋玉盤,	[As if] millions of golden bells spin on the jade plate,
醉客滿船皆暫醒。	Drunk guests on the boat all become momentarily sober.

(Chinese from ctext[8]; tr. Sun 2012: 82)

Yuan certainly knew that the *pipa* was absent from the classics. Though it had been adopted into the *qingshang* ensemble, unlike the more foreign-seeming

---

[7] Chinese Text Project: https://ctext.org/text.pl?node=187262&if=en.
[8] Chinese Text Project: https://ctext.org/text.pl?node=187421&if=en.

Kuchean *pipa*, Yuan's other poems tend to extol mainly instruments mentioned in classical sources. However, he must have recognized that the expressive potential of the *pipa*, as depicted here, was in alignment with classical principles of musical expression and power, not mere showmanship. Its evocative sound even merited a comparison with one of the most prestigious of classical instruments, the stone chime, sounded from within the palace.

But it was precisely this power that unnerved Yuan when it was wielded by Xuanzong without caution. The clearest example of this was the clouded judgment Xuanzong displayed regarding his concubine Yang Guifei and An Lushan 安禄山 (c. 703–57; probable Sogdian name Roχšan), the general of Sogdian-Göktürk descent who delighted him with their skill at a dance of Sogdian origin, the "whirling dance," before leading a rebellion that put the empire into turmoil. In the next section, we explore this dance, alongside another dance of Sogdian origin with which it may have been confused, the "leaping dance." The two dances seem to have been known in the Sogdian community in Chang'an for some time, below the awareness of court circles, and also betray connections much further afield in time and space.

3 Dancing "Sogdian Style": The *Huxuanwu* and the *Hutengwu*

Together with the foreign instruments and courtly performing divisions, two dances associated with the area of Sogdiana/Kangju 康居 (by and large modern Uzbekistan and Tajikistan), the *huxuanwu* 胡旋舞 (the whirling dance) and the *hutengwu* 胡腾舞 (the leaping dance), were part of the strong foreign, cultural presence in cosmopolitan Tang Chang'an, as well as the object of perennial condemnations by conservative courtly factions of that very cosmopolitanism.

This last point is very much evident in a pair of poems entitled the "The Hu Whirling Girls" (*Huxuan nü* 胡旋女), where Yuan Zhen and his friend Bai Juyi remark upon the courtly fascination with the Sogdian whirling dance, the *huxuanwu*. As corroborated by a passage in the *Old Book of Tang*, An Lushan was a superb dancer who "in the presence of the emperor Xuanzong performed the *huxuanwu* with movements as swift as those of a whirlwind" (*Jiu Tangshu* 133: 5368; tr. Zhang 2005: 94; ctext 213.7[9]). He is the same An Lushan who in 755 would lead an enormously disruptive rebellion against the emperor. Yuan and Bai were both born after the rebellion had collapsed, so, while their accounts are not necessarily reliable as historical sources, they nevertheless illustrate the ways in which the framing of the Sogdian music and dance in favor at the Tang court

---

[9] Chinese Text Project: https://ctext.org/wiki.pl?if=gb&chapter=944936.

interacted with the historiography of events. Yuan Zhen – strongly hostile to the Hu and their cultural influence on Tang life – declared that the *huxuanwu*, the whirling dance, was distracting the emperor from his duties, attracting the focus of all those in court following the emperor's lead, and thus being a kind of a Hu conspiracy in preparation for An Lushan's rebellion, a position that may very well reflect Tang ethnic discourses characterized by what Abramson termed "stereotype of the untrustworthy other" (Abramson 2007: 38):

天寶欲末胡欲亂。	With the Tianbao era [742–55] drawing to a close, the Hu were ready to rebel.
胡人獻女能胡旋。	[Hence] the Hu presented to the throne the Hu whirling girls.
旋得明王不覺迷,	The girls whirled and whirled 'til the wise Monarch was infatuated,
妖胡奄到長生殿。	And the demon Hu came right to the [inner] Palace of Long Life.
寄言旋目與旋心,	Let me tell those whirling with their eyes and their hearts:
有國有家當其譴。	You ought to be condemned by all who cherish family and the land.

(Chinese from ctext[10]; tr. Chen 2012: 173–74)

Bai Juyi, himself of Central Asian ancestry and whose family had maintained distinctive non-Chinese traits (Chen 2012: 162), avoids in his reply-poem the term 'hu' in any pejorative sense, and points to the existence of the dance long before An Lushan's rebellion, asking the dancers to enlighten the illustrious monarch:

胡旋女，出康居，	*Sogdian whirling girl* [*huxuan nü*], you came from Sogdiana [Kangju 康居].
徒勞東來萬里餘。	In vain did you labor to come east more than 10,000 miles.
中原自有胡旋者，	*For in the central plains there were already some who could do the Sogdian whirl*
...	
天寶季年時欲變，	In the closing years of the Tianbao era, the times were about to change,

[10] Chinese Text Project: https://ctext.org/text.pl?node=187286&if=en.

(cont.)

臣妾人人學圜轉。	Officials and concubines all learned how to circle and turn:
中有太真外祿山，	Within the palace was the favorite Precious Consort Yang [i.e. Yang Guifei], without was Roxshan [i.e. An Lushan]
二人最道能胡旋。	The two were most highly acclaimed for being able to do the Hu Whirling Dance.
胡旋女，莫空舞，	Sogdian whirling girls, don't dance to no purpose;
數唱此歌悟明主。	Sing this song several times to enlighten our illustrious sovereign.

(Chinese from ctext[11]; tr. Mair 1994: 486, slightly emended and emphasis added)

Notwithstanding the more positive angle toward this foreign cultural marker and its potential impact upon the fate of the empire, what is also remarkable about Bai's poem is that it provides a vivid description of the sonic component of the dance – strings and drums – as well as some of its distinctive choreographic details:

胡旋女，胡旋女，	Sogdian whirling girl, Sogdian whirling girl –
心應弦，手應鼓。	Her heart answers to the strings, Her hands answer to the drums.
弦鼓一聲雙袖舉，	*At the sound of the strings and drums, she raises her arms,*
回雪飄飄轉蓬舞。	*Like swirling snowflakes tossed about, she turns in her twirling dance.*
左旋右轉不知疲，	*Whirling to the left, turning to the right, she never feels exhausted,*
千匝萬周無已時。	*A thousand rounds, 10,000 circuits – it never seems to end.*
人間物類無可比，	Among men and living creatures, she is peerless;
奔車輪緩旋風遲。	*Compared to her, the wheels of a racing chariot revolve slowly and a whirlwind is sluggish.*

(Chinese from ctext (see n. 11); tr. Mair 1994: 486; emphasis added)

A type of ekphrasis if you will, this segment of the poem, with its vivid and almost visceral description of the whirling dancer, may very well have triggered

---

[11] Chinese Text Project: https://ctext.org/text.pl?node=188705&if=en.

an empathetic physical response on the part of the reader. It is as verbally suggestive as some of the numerous depictions of the dance in Tang art – with their flowing ribbons and gracefully pirouetting bodies of the dancers – are visually commanding. Particularly arresting, for example, is the early Tang depiction of the dance featured in the representation of the Healing Ritual in the *Bhaiṣajya-guru Sutra* on the north wall of Cave 220 in Dunhuang, dating from 642. Two pairs of female dancers, caught in mid-motion, are flanked by two seemingly multiethnic ensembles consisting of assorted drums and a transverse flute on the left, and a similar percussion ensemble together with one lute and a couple of more flutes on the right.[12] As scholars have convincingly argued (Ning 2004: 123–26; Sha 2013), the large scene of whirling dances and instrumental music is not even recorded as part of the healing ritual in the text of the sutra. In fact, according to Ning, the musical scene corresponds to contemporaneous literary descriptions of female dancers and musicians performing during the celebrations of the Lantern Festival in Chang'an, a fact that renders the scene reminiscent of urban New Year festivities. Since the cave dates from the early Tang period, the incorporation of the dance into what very likely is court-related iconography corroborates Bai Juyi's post-rebellion testimony that the *huxuanwu* had been part of the courtly celebrations at the Tang court long before Emperor Xuanzong's reign.

In addition to the realm of poetry, a number of references appear in official dynastic histories, which not only underscore the "foreignness" of the *huxuanwu,* but also help shed light upon some of the mechanisms through which it became solidly entrenched in the Tang world. One of the earliest such references, for example, comes from the biography of Wu Yanxiu 武延秀 (d. 710) as recorded in the *Old Book of Tang* 舊唐書 (*Jiu Tangshu* 183: 4733; cited in Zhang 2005: 94; ctext 187.43[13]). Wu Yanxiu was the grandnephew of Empress Wu Zetian 武則天, who sent him in 698 to marry the daughter of the khan of the Second Turkic Empire, Bäkçor Qapağan of the clan Ašina (r. 692-716). While the marriage never took place, the khan detained Wu Yanxiu until 703, when he allowed him to return to China. Back at the Tang court, Wu Yanxiu sang Turkic songs and performed the *huxuan* dance to the enchantment of his audience (Zhang 2005: 94).

Other passages reference tributes sent to the Tang court which often included whirling dancing girls. As recorded in the *New Book of Tang* (*Xin Tangshu* 新唐書, 1060), for example, the tribute sent from Sogdiana in 713 consisted of armors, crystal cups, ostrich eggs, and whirling girls (*huxuan*

---

[12] Dunhuang, Cave 220, Main Chamber, North Wall: Digital Dunhuang (www.e-dunhuang.com/cave/ 10.0001/0001.0001.0220).

[13] Chinese Text Project: https://ctext.org/wiki.pl?if=gb&chapter=173483.

nü), among other items (*Xin Tangshu* 221B: 6244; cited in Zhang 2005: 94; ctext 146.3[14]). This was certainly not a one-time event since, according to the *Cefu Yuangui* 冊府元龜 ("Archival Palace as the Great Oracle", compiled 1013), between 720 and 751, several envoys from different locations in Sogdiana – such as Samarkand, Kesh (modern Shahr-i Sabz), and Maimurgh (either Kuldortepa in the Middle Zeravshan Valley, or Panjikent) – brought to the Tang court cheetahs and equally valuable dancing girls (*huxuan nü*) (Watt 2004: 307). In fact, with the notable exceptions of Wu Yanxiu and An Lushan – both male and both Tang cultural insiders – the Sogdian *huxuan* performers in the context of courtly entertainment are consistently identified in Chinese records as female; similarly, whirling dancers in court-related Sui and Tang iconography are predominantly female as well. That said, there does exist some evidence to suggest that this gendering of the *huxuanwu* might have been far less constricted outside the courtly domain (see, for example, the dancers on temple doors from circa 700 in Juliano & Lerner 2001: 250).

Imports from Sogdiana, however, also included what seem to have been exclusively male dances, such as the *hutengwu* (胡騰舞) or the "leaping dance." The *hutengwu* was likely first introduced to China during the Northern Wei (386–535) and seems to have been linked to the consumption of grape-wine, which became quite common during the Tang when China started to import this kind of wine from Central Asia (Schafer 1963: 142). While mentions of this dance in the dynastic histories are extremely rare, the *hutengwu*, just like the *huxuanwu*, is referenced in Tang poetry. In his *Night Viewing of the Hu Leaping Dance at the Palace Assistant Secretary Mr. Wang's Residence* (*Wang zhongcheng zhai ye guan wu huteng* 王中丞宅夜观舞胡騰), for example, Liu Yanshi 劉言史 (742–813) recounts a private night gathering of literati, where a young male from the Shi State 石國 (Tashkent) danced the *hutengwu* with rapid movements to the accompaniment of a transverse flute (*hengdi* 橫笛) and lute (*pipa* 琵琶) (*Quan Tang shi/Complete Tang Poems*, 14.468: 5323; cited in Zhang 2005: 93):

石國胡兒人見少，	People rarely see a barbarian of the Shi State;
蹲舞尊前急如鳥。	Dancing in front of the banquet, [his movement] is as swift as a bird.

---

[14] Chinese Text Project: https://ctext.org/wiki.pl?if=gb&chapter=976168#p4.

(cont.)

織成蕃帽虛頂尖,	The woven barbarian hat is of a pointed top;
細氎胡衫雙袖小。	The barbarian jacket, made of refined cotton, has two narrow sleeves.
手中抛下蒲萄盞,	His hand drops the wine cup;
西顧忽思鄉路遠。	He looks into the west, suddenly thinks of the distanced road to his hometown.
跳身轉轂寶帶鳴,	He jumps like a rolling wheel and his precious belt sounds;
弄腳繽紛錦靴軟。	His feet move vivaciously and his boots are soft.
橫笛琵琶遍頭促。	A bamboo flute and a *pipa* with a tilted head,
亂騰新毯雪朱毛,	He jumps energetically on the new carpet of snowy and crimson fur.

(Chinese from ctext[15]; tr. Sha 2016: 28)

The *huteng* dancer in Li Duan's 李端 (743–82) poem *The Leaping Hu* (*Huteng'er* 胡騰兒) is a young male from Liangzhou (where Sogdians are known to have settled from at least 227 CE); he has skin pale (or smooth) like jade and a sizeable nose (which clearly points to a non-Han physiognomy) (*Quan Tang shi* 9.284: 3238; cited in Zhang 2005: 94). Like his counterpart from Tashkent in Liu Yanshi's poem, he dances at a private night banquet and wears soft boots and a beaded hat (for the different shapes of Sogdian hats, see Yatsenko 2012: 109). As part of his dancing, he fakes drunkenness while maintaining a rhythmically perfect step with arms akimbo. A song of the *qin* zither (the iconic instrument of the Chinese literati) concludes the whole act.

揚眉動目踏花氈,	He lifts his eyebrows, moves his eyes, and steps on the flowery carpet;
紅汗交流珠帽偏。	He sweats heavily and his pearl hat inclines aside.
醉卻東傾又西倒,	He [seems to be] drunk, teetering towards the east and then the west;
雙靴柔弱滿燈前。	His boots are softly [wandering] in front of the lamps.
環行急蹴皆應節,	He walks in a circle or treads fast, all conforming to the beat;

---

[15] Chinese Text Project: https://ctext.org/text.pl?node=200082&if=en.

(cont.)

反手叉腰如卻月。	He puts his hands reversely on his waist, like a semicircular moon.
絲桐忽奏一曲終,	Suddenly, the zither [*sitong* 絲桐, i.e. *qin*] plays to an end;

(Chinese from ctext;[16] tr. Sha 2016: 30)

It appears that such dancing was often performed in the local taverns as well and this, combined with the fact that wine shops in China were frequently run by Sogdians, may have led to the "drunken barbarian" stock character found not only in China but also in the Japanese courtly cultures. One of the characters in the *gigaku* 伎樂 plays – a form of dance-theatre that, according to tradition, was imported to Japan from China in 612 (see Section 4, p. 47) – is, for example, identified as Suiko-ō 醉胡王 ("Drunken Barbarian King"). This was possibly a character in the "Drunken Barbarians" piece who, according to the thirteenth-century *Kyōkunshō* 教訓抄 ("Annotated Teaching"), was performing a drunken-dance and wearing a head-mask with "Sogdian" cap and stereotypical large nose (Figure 2).

As we have seen, the preponderance of evidence seems to indicate so far that the *huxuanwu* was customarily performed by female dancers, particularly at the court or court-organized festivities, where the flashiness of their whirling together with their ribbons and colorful costumes contributed to the fastuous image of the banquets. On the other hand, as encountered chiefly in Tang poetry, the *hutengwu* – with its young male dancers dressed in rather unassuming attire and with choreography filled with connotation of wine and drunkenness – seems to have been better suited to the kind of private entertainment often reserved for night gatherings of *literati* or urban taverns. Indeed, depictions of the *hutengwu* in such settings became extremely popular from the Northern Dynasties (386–581) onward and are found on a wide range of artifacts: ceramics, jade ornaments, silverware, and even tomb mural paintings, sarcophagi, and funerary couches. The iconography of the dance is consistent in that it encapsulates its most distinctive elements: the leaping, the squatting, and particularly the holding of the arms above the head with interlaced fingers (Figure 3).

---

[16] Chinese Text Project: https://ctext.org/text.pl?node=163583&if=en.

Figure 2 Gigaku Mask, Suiko-ō ("Drunken Barbarian King"). Asuka period, seventh century. Tokyo National Museum N-219. Source: ColBase: Integrated Collections Database of the National Institutes for Cultural Heritage, Japan (https://colbase.nich.go.jp/collection_items/tnm/N-219?locale=en).

In every significant way, each and all these distinctive features connect the *hutengwu* to a type of dance long known in the larger Iranian cultural ecumene, and thus in Sogdiana (Lo Muzio, in press). As depicted on Greek vases and Achaemenid artifacts from the late sixth century to the end of the fourth century BCE, such a dance – possibly to be identified with the Greek *oklasma* – was performed in a majority of cases by dancers in standard Asiatic attire, including the characteristic Phrygian cap and often in what is thought to be Dionysiac setting (Figure 4 and the fourth-century *lebes gamikos* in the British Museum[17]). Several more recent examples from Gandhāra (today's northern Pakistan and adjacent areas) attest to the eastward dissemination of the dance before the middle of the first millennium CE (Lo Muzio 2019). Whatever the prehistory of the *hutengwu* may ultimately prove to be, and although there are no known representations of it in the art from Sogdiana proper, this dance is represented with a remarkable degree of consistency on artifacts that predate our Tang literary reference. In particular, most

---

[17] BM 1772,0320.468: www.britishmuseum.org/collection/object/G_1772-0320-468.

Figure 3 Sogdian dancer. Plaque from pagoda of Xiudingsi 修定寺 temple on
Mount Qingliang 清凉, Tang dynasty (618–907). The Cleveland Museum of
Art. Gift of C. T. Loo 1921.263. Creative Commons (CC0 1.0).

such documentation associates it with Sogdians in China, not only as performers
belonging to those communities, but also as patrons.

   To this effect, among the most important such witnesses are some late sixth-
century stone furniture items from tombs of Sogdians buried in China, a good
number of which were found near Chang'an. Known as the great traders of
Inner Asia, the Sogdians were the Iranian-speaking intermediaries of commercial exchanges in Central Asia, the steppes, and China especially between the
fifth and the eighth centuries CE; between the fifth and the sixth centuries they
settled in significant numbers in China (La Vaissière 2005; Trombert & La
Vassière 2005; Rong 2018). To date, we know of roughly a dozen examples
from the final decades of the Northern Dynasties and the beginning of the Sui
Dynasty (Cheng 2010: 86–87). The images carved on the panels of these
sarcophagi or funerary couches have excited a high degree of interest on the
part of scholars, since they feature complex imagery related to Chinese,
Zoroastrian, and possibly Buddhist and Manichean traditions, as well as

Figure 4 Dancer (with "Phrygian" cap?). Chalcedony scaraboid.
Achaemenid period (c. 400 BCE). The J. Paul Getty Museum
81.AN.76.88. (Creative Commons 4.0 International/CC BY 4.0)

music-making and dancing activities (e.g. Juliano & Lerner 1997; Lerner 2005, 2011; Grenet, Riboud & Yang 2004). Insofar as dancers are concerned, most of the depictions on these funerary artifacts feature male performers, and most of them dance the *hutengwu* in the context of what appear to be private parties under the patronage of the deceased. The only depiction of what was clearly not a leaping but a whirling dance – performed in this instance by a male rather than the customary female dancer of the Tang period – is found on the sarcophagus of Yu Hong 虞弘 (d. 592), in a setting similar to that found in Tang textual and visual records, that of a court-like event with musicians flanking the whirling dancer (Cao 2013: panel 5, p. 48–49).

The *hutengwu* dancers are depicted in this Sogdian funerary art in a remarkably consistent manner. Let us consider, for example, two of the panels that form the long side of the funerary couch of An Jia 安伽 (518–79), leader of the Sogdian community in the city of Tongzhou 同州 (near Chang'an), who likely traced his ancestry to the Sogdian state of Bukhara (Figures 5a and 5b). Each of the two panels

(a)   (b)

Figure 5 *Hutengwu* dancer. Panels from An Jia's funerary couch (581 CE). Shaanxi Provincial Institute of Archaeology, Xi'an, PRC). Source: Gabriela Currie.

features a male dancer performing the *hutengwu* – and not the "whirling dance" as generally assumed by art historians (e.g. Juliano & Lerner 2001: 58). He is dressed in a rather unassuming attire and wears boots, just like in the descriptions we found in the Tang poems; he has his hands clasped above his head and has a bent knee as if launching into or landing from a leap. All these identifiers – male dancer, attire, clasped hands, etc. – are also present in the banquet scenes depicted panels from other funerary couches, such as those housed today at the Musée Guimet (Delacour & Riboud 2004: fig. 20) and Miho Museum (Miho Museum 1997: 253), as well as on the Anyang panel held at the Boston Museum of Fine Arts.[18]

---

[18] MFA 12.589 (left side, middle register): https://collections.mfa.org/download/12931; jsessionid=0C97ACDD4117E87D9668C42137C66426.

The composition of the musical accompaniment in the scene, however, is not as consistent as one might expect. In the An Jia panels, the group surrounding the *huteng* dancer contains no musicians, but some of the individuals appear to be clapping, thus creating an aural rhythmic background to the dance. The upper registers of both panels feature the party entourage proper provided also with musicians playing harp (*konghou*), lute (*pipa*), and (on the right panel) panpipes (*paixiao*): this placement of the instruments, however, suggests that they are not part of the soundtrack of the dance proper. In other instances, the instrumental accompaniment varies quite dramatically, both in terms of the composition and size. The Musée Guimet panel, for example, features a lute and a transverse flute (exactly as in Liu Yanshi's poem quoted earlier in this section), while the Miho panel showcases two relatively large ensembles that flank that dancer and consist of two lutes on each side, accompanied by a harp and a transverse flute on the left and two flutes and cymbals on the right. It does seem, therefore, that if the iconography of the scenes is to be trusted, the stable elements are associated with the dance proper while the variable is the composition of the instrumental accompaniment, which might reflect performative flexibility.

The dance imagery associated with pre-Tang Sogdian tomb furniture seems to indicate, therefore, that the association of the *huxuanwu* with courtly entertainment and of the *hutengwu* with private gatherings might indeed predate the Tang era, but that, ultimately, it was during Tang that the courtly *huxuanwu* came to be performed exclusively by female dancers while the *hutengwu* remained in the male performative domain.

The insider views of the Sogdian community in Chang'an afforded by these visual works contrasts strongly with the view presented in the official Chinese sources. We have seen, of course, that the whirling dance captivated the outsiders at court much more than the leaping dance, though both were included in the dance type known in the sources as the "strong dance" (*jianwu* 健舞), as distinct from "soft dances" (*ruanwu* 软舞) in a typology that, though from the Tang, recalls the classical antecedent of military and civic dances (*wuwu* 武舞 and *wenwu* 文舞) (Gimm 1966: 255). The idea of performative flexibility suggested by the unusual selection of instruments in the panels, though no doubt the consequence of limited resources and, potentially, organological preferences within the Sogdian community, contrasts so strongly with the fixity of the court ensembles and their rigid ordering of performances. It reminds us of the extent to which different kinds of sources provide windows into the actions of such different communities using similar artforms and within the same city. But what happens in a community with little written record? In the next section we turn to such a community: Kucha.

4 The Western Regions: Kucha

For the better part of the first millennium CE, the oasis-kingdom of Kucha (in present-day Xinjiang, China) was one of the major Buddhist centers on the northern branch of the Silk Road trade routes straddling the Tarim basin (see Rhie 2002: 578–719 for a good introduction to the history and art of the kingdom). The native language of the kingdom, known as Kuchean, together with that of the neighboring kingdom of Agni, belonged to the Tocharian family of the *centum* branch of Indo-European languages and were spoken along a stretch of the northern Tarim Basin between Aksu and Turfan. Little is known about the Kuchean musical world in the second part of the first millennium CE, and even less about how this world took part in the larger network of Eurasian musical exchanges. Several important studies, however, have long demonstrated that in many respects, the Kuchean musical practices of this time had a great role in shaping Chinese courtly musical life during the Sui and Tang dynasties, when its musical repertoires, respected musicians, and valued musical instruments found their way into the imperial environment (e.g. Liu 1969; Zeng 2003; see also, Section 2 of this Element). By the turn of the seventh century, for example, musicians from Kucha and other kingdoms of the Tarim Basin had traveled to, or had been in the employment of, the Chinese imperial court for quite some time (Liu 1969: 103–7; Picken & Nickson 2000: 205–6). Bai Mingda 白明達 and Bai Zhitong 白智通 (from Kucha) and Pei Shenfu 裴神符 (from Kashgar) were among the most famous, and the latter is even credited with introducing a different way of playing the *pipa* (plucking the strings with his fingers rather than strumming them with a plectrum). Instruments of likely Kuchean provenance, such as the so-called "Kuchean *pipa*" (*wuxian*), the "wether drum" (*jiegu*), and maybe even the *bili*, were already solidly established in the courtly Chinese instrumentarium by the Sui dynasty.

The encounters between the Kuchean and Chinese musical worlds go well beyond circulation of musical instruments, repertoires, or even musicians. The *Book of Sui* (*Suishu* 隋書, completed 636), provides one extraordinary account of the meeting between two widely different music-theoretical conceptualizations. This famous musical encounter took place during the Xianbei Northern Zhou dynasty (557–81 CE) in the aftermath of the marriage in 568 CE of the Göktürk princess from the Ašina clan to the Northern Zhou Emperor Wu, and brought face to face elements of the South Asian and Chinese music-theoretical contemporaneous traditions. According to the account, the Ašina princess and future empress had in her retinue musicians from Kang (Samarkand), Qiuci (Kucha), and other places; the *Old Book of Tang* adds musicians from Shule (Kashgar) and An (Bukhara) (Liu 1958: 466–67). One of these musicians coming from Kucha was a player of the *hu-pipa* 胡琵琶 (probably a five-string *pipa*) named Sujiva (the name is recorded as Suzhipo 蘇祇婆 in the Chinese source). A master player of the instrument and the son of a master-musician, which suggests a hereditary tradition, Sujiva demonstrated to his Chinese counterparts at the imperial court a set of seven "Western modes and tones" on his instrument. The substance of this demonstration was later invoked by eyewitness Zheng Yi 鄭譯 (540–91) – a distinguished statesman and music connoisseur who was himself a skilled *pipa*-player – in the context of the series of conferences convened by the emperor between 582 and 594 with the aim of rectifying the official system of imperial ritual music (see p. 9). Apparently, therefore, the original encounter in 568 CE triggered a process through which Kuchean music conceptualizations were adapted to, and subsequently integrated into, Chinese musical thought (Picken & Nickson 2000: 206–18). Sujiva's "modes and tones" were heavily contingent upon South Asian music-theoretical lore, in particular the roughly contemporaneous Sanskrit music-theoretical terminology as transmitted by the seventh-century South Indian Kuḍumiyāmalai inscription. Of the seven Sanskrit equivalents featured in the *Book of Sui*, five of these terms (*Sādhārita, Kaiśika, Saḍjagrāma, Ṣaḍava,* and *Pañcama*) refer to the primary *grāmarāgas* (melody-types) while two (*Ṣāḍjī* and *Ārṣabhī*) may relate to two of the *jātis* (modal patterns) (Widdess 1995: 15–16). Zheng Yi realized that the seven modes could be mapped onto the seven notes in the Chinese scale. With this insight, he could set each of those seven modes on the twelve fixed pitches of Chinese music theory and realize a system of eighty-four modes (Picken 2000: 206, 210). This system of eighty-four modes went on to become a standard feature of the music theory of the Tang and later dynasties (Pian 1967: 43–47). While some scholars see this as an "excellent example of direct 'diffusionist' transmission of musical knowledge" (Picken 2000: 206), such an approach leaves little room for Kuchean agency. The Kuchean "seven Western modes" are neither direct links to, nor unmediated derivatives of, contemporaneous Indian musical modal conceptualizations. Rather, they must be understood as a possible expression of a multivalent local musical culture belonging to a kingdom-oasis that – as a node of cultural encounters and disper-sals – functioned as a redistribution point in the Eurasian network of musical exchanges. Kuchean music iconography and terminology can give us an even better sense of that role.

4.1 The Kizil Caves

As rich as the information the Chinese sources provide regarding Kuchean musical practices and customs may be, they nevertheless reflect in large part a sense of the exotic, the foreign, and at times the coveted cosmopolitanism that characterized the Chinese perception of cultural life of the Western Regions. Information provided by local Kuchean sources contributes to a more complete picture of the kingdom's place in the larger network of Eurasian musical exchanges. Most relevant for our present purposes are local iconographic and linguistic sources: depictions of musical instruments in the complex of Buddhist caves at Kizil, and some music terminology culled from the surviving corpus of fragmentary texts in Kuchean language. Together they portray a musical culture that was not merely an important source of musical practices, objects, and lore for Sui and Tang China, but also, and more importantly, a critical node in the vast network of Eurasian transcultural musical commerce linking Western, Central, Southern, and Eastern Asia.

The construction of the Buddhist caves of the Kizil complex northwest of Kucha proper began sometime in the fourth century and lasted until the eighth century. A hundred or so of these caves have relatively well-preserved murals. While Gandhāran, Indian, and Sassanian stylistic and iconographic traits are noticeable in the Kizil paintings throughout this period, during the last phase of artistic production (the mid-sixth to mid-seventh century) there are also signs of influence from the Sogdians, the Middle Iranian group who had their cultural center in the region of Samarkand (present-day Uzbekistan) and inhabited various settlements in the Tarim Basin as well. In the fifty or so caves at Kizil inventoried by Yao Shihong 姚士宏, the murals feature a plethora of musical instruments known to have originated from locations across Eurasia, from Sassanian Iran to China, including: angular and arched harps, four- and five-stringed lutes, moon-lutes, panpipes, vertical- and side-blown flutes, and a large variety of percussion instruments (Yao 1983).

Insofar as the types of harp are concerned, the depictions at Kizil are heavily weighted toward the arched harp. This is an instrument whose neck extends from and forms a bow-shaped curve with the body, was historically most intimately associated with the South Asian instrumentarium, and was closely linked with Buddhism (Figure 6). Before the first millennium CE, arched harps are attested only on the Indian subcontinent; some of the earliest-known depictions of the instrument appear in Bharhut (Madhya Pradesh), for example, while later representations come from Sanchi (Madhya Pradesh) and Mathura (Uttar Pradesh), among other sites. From South Asia, the arched harp spread mainly eastward and is found depicted in the earliest murals at Kizil (fourth century CE). Its dominant presence in the Kizil murals attests that the arched harp very quickly became an integral part of local iconography and possibly the local instrumentarium. Moreover, in later centuries two morphologically different types of arched harps are represented at Kizil – one known from Indian

Figure 6 Musician plying an arched harp. Butkara, Pakistan, first century CE.
Museo Nazionale d'Arte Orientale, Rome, Italy. Inv. 1144 (detail). Source:
Gabriela Currie

iconography and one seemingly indigenous – which suggests that, while the
Indian version of the instrument continued to be part of Kuchean culture (at
least iconographically), local artists generated morphological changes that
possibly aligned it more closely with Kuchean practices and aesthetics (Li
Mei 2014: 49–54). Images of arched harps still abound in the Kizil caves of
the seventh and even eighth centuries, which makes Kucha one of the last
significant iconographic outposts of an instrument emblematic of Indian
musical culture, since the arched harp seems to have vanished almost completely from the Indian pictorial record after the Guptas (275–590).

The depictions of the angular harps in the Kizil murals, by contrast, point toward
a different cultural alignment. Characteristic of the Western Asian regions and
particularly Iran (Lawergren 2010: 119), the angular harp is an instrument in which
the neck forms a clear angle with the resonator (Figure 7). It enjoyed a very stable
construction until around the mid-sixth century, traveled eastward to China, but
almost completely bypassed the South Asian subcontinent. The earliest textual
Chinese references to the angular harp (*konghou*) appeared late during the Han
dynasty (206 BCE–220 CE), and the instrument develops culturally specific morphological traits over the next several centuries. While most of the angular harps
depicted in Kuchean art belong to the West Asian type, some depictions from the
eighth century and later manifest Chinese morphological traits common during the

Figure 7 Musician playing an angular harp. Figurine in a polychrome women's orchestra from Zhang Sheng's 張盛 tomb (Anyang, Henan Province, PRC). Sui Dynasty (581–618). Henan Museum, Zhengzhou, Henan Province, PRC.
Source: Gabriela Currie

Tang dynasty, such as those found at the Kumtura caves (c. 25 km west of Kucha), among other sites (Li Mei 2014: 46). The presence of two types of angular harps, one with Western Asian and the other with Chinese morphological elements, raises therefore the possibility that the Kuchean iconography reflects two different waves of organological adoption: the earlier one from the Iranian lands to the west (whether directly or indirectly), and the later one from the late Tang China to the east.

The other category of string instruments depicted in the Kizil caves – from the earliest times and even more often than either one of the harps – is the almond-shaped, short-necked lute in its two morphological configurations: lutes with bent necks and four strings (Figure 8), and lutes with straight necks and five strings (Figure 9). The four-stringed with bent neck Chinese *pipa* (distinguished

Figure 8 Musician playing a four-string *pipa* with bent neck. Figurine in a polychrome women's orchestra from Zhang Sheng's tomb (Anyang, Henan Province, PRC). Sui Dynasty (581–618). Henan Museum, Zhengzhou, Henan Province, PRC. Source: Gabriela Currie

in Chinese as the *quxiang pipa* 曲項琵琶) descends from Western and Central Asian prototypes and is related to the Iranian *barbat* (Kishibe 1940; Picken 1955). It likely entered China in the third century, and some of its earliest depictions appear during the subsequent Northern Wei Dynasty (386–534 CE) in the Yungang caves (Shanxi, China). The prototype for the East Asian five-stringed and straight-neck lute (Ch. *wuxian pipa*) comes most likely from the South Asian subcontinent, where some of the best iconographic representations date from the second to the fourth century CE at Amaravati in Andhra Pradesh.

The representations of these two instruments in Kizil are heavily weighted in favor of the five-stringed straight-neck type, which appears fifty times, while the four-string bent-neck variant appears only twenty-five times (Yao 1983). Moreover, the two types of lutes are most often depicted separately, almost never in the same scene, and in very few instances in the same cave. This iconographic predilection seems to reflect local performing habits, since it stands in stark contrast to that observed in the Dunhuang murals of the Sui and Tang dynasties, where the two instruments are consistently depicted together as part of orchestras representative of contemporaneous Chinese courtly practices, as well as in the written evidence of these ensembles (cf. Table 2, p. 13–15). The

Figure 9 Musician playing five-string *pipa* with straight neck. Figurine in
a polychrome women's orchestra from Zhang Sheng's tomb (Anyang, Henan
Province, China). Sui Dynasty (581–618). Henan Museum, Zhengzhou, Henan
Province, PCR. Source: Gabriela Currie

popularity of the five-stringed lute in the Kuchean iconographic tradition under-
scores the crucial position the kingdom-oasis held in the eastward dissemination
of this instrument, as the lone node through which it entered China.

4.2 The Subashi *Sarira*

The chronology of the adoption of different types of harps and lutes in the
representations of the Buddhist caves at Kizil suggests that Kucha was a crucial
node in the circulation of musical instruments during the first millennium CE.
There are also local visual representations of music-making that demonstrate an
equally pluralistic musical life, one that drew and subsequently affected far-
flung cultures through Eurasian exchange networks. One such example is the
famous *sarira* (funerary box) currently in the Tokyo National Museum (TC
557).[19] It was found at the beginning of the twentieth century at Subashi, the
Buddhist monastic complex north of Kucha proper, and dated to the sixth or
early seventh century, the very period when Kuchean music and musicians were

---

[19] Tokyo National Museum: www.tnm.jp/modules/r_collection/index.php?controller=
other&colid=TC557&t=type&id=45.

all the rage at the Chinese imperial courts (for a recent music-iconographical study, see Currie 2020). Depicted on its drum is a long procession of dancers and musicians.

The dancers wear extravagant, richly colored, and exquisitely cut costumes, and two of them wear full-head animal masks resembling a black-dog and Garuda, while the rest wear full-head humanoid masks that – together with vestments and accoutrements – seem to reference distinct ethnic groups. Three dancers have almond-shaped eyes, Indo-European features, and a crown of the Sassanian type (Tocharians? Sogdians?), while one dancer has a long moustache, shaved head, and Turkic couture. This variety of physical features and clothing is very much in line with the multiethnic population of Kucha at the time. Sogdian merchants mingled with local Tocharians and the local ethnic fabric may also have included Turkic elements since at that time the Kuchean kings had already recognized the Western khagans as their overlords, and, as we have already seen, in 568 several local musicians had been chosen to be part of the Turkic princess' retinue for her wedding to the Northern Zhou emperor (see p. 38).

The musicians wear costumes that are strikingly similar to those of the so-called "Tocharian Knights (Princes)," the four male figures with reddish hair and light-colored eyes depicted in the Cave of the Sixteen Sword-Bearers (Kizil Cave 8) dated 432–38 (Figure 10). They play different instruments of both West and East Asian provenance such as an angular harp, panpipes, and a variety of drums (single- and double-headed drums, as well as frame drums and a beautiful ornate barrel-drum).

Scholars have long noted that the population in Kucha performed a so-called *sumozhe* 蘇摩遮 festival, which may have coincided with the New Year's celebrations, where musicians and dancers wore animal and humanoid masks (e.g. Pelliot 1932; Gaulier 1973; Compareti & Cristoforetti 2007). Its Kuchean roots – albeit roots formed at the intersection of numerous West, Central, and East Asian celebrations of renewal – were acknowledged in two ninth-century sources from the late Tang era. The monk Huilin 慧琳 (fl. 810) in his *Yiqiejing yinyi* 一切經音義 ("Sound and Meaning of all Sutras") explains that *sumozhe* comes from Kucha and that when it takes place residents wear animal masks and shake their heads (Wang-Toutain 1996: 86). Duan Chengshi 段成式 (800–863) tells us that inhabitants in Kucha wear dog head-masks and monkey face-masks during the celebrations of the first day of the (Chinese) New Year and that men and women dance and sing day and night (Liu 1969: 170).

The *sumozhe* could be related to festivals of renewal celebrated across Eurasia, from Japan to the Abbasid court. For example, Norman H. Rothschild engaged in a fascinating recent study of the complex history

Figure 10 Donor portraits. Cave of the Sixteen Sword Bearers, Kizil, seventh century. Berlin: MIK III 8426a–c. Source: Le Coq 1924, *Die Buddhistische Spätantike in Mittelasien*, vol. 4, Pl. 4.

of this dance with masks and music in Tang China in the context of the larger Eurasian name-related masked performances (Chinese, Sanskrit, Arabic, etc.), and convincingly argued that the *sumozhe* was part of the performance of the "cold-splashing Sogdian plays" which took place in the first half of the eighth century (Rothschild 2017). With regard to the style of music that might have accompanied the Chinese as well as possibly the Kuchean performances, Laurence Picken points out that a group of Tang-era mouth organ tunes, including a *sumozhe* melody, manifest "consistent syncopated isorhythmic patterns [that] might indicate a Sogdian (and ultimately Indian) origin" (Picken 1969:80). Most likely from China and possibly through Korea, the *somakusa* 蘇莫者 was introduced to Japan to be celebrated by musicians and dancers wearing animal and monster masks (Eckardt 1953), and intersects in different ways with both the *gigaku* and *bugaku* 舞樂 dance traditions (discussed in Ortolani 1995: 29–37 and 39–53, respectively). The *gigaku,* the earlier kind of such masked dances, was said to have originated in Kashgar (western end of the Tarim basin) (Rosenfield 1968: 10); in 562, an envoy brought back to Japan objects related to the *gigaku*, probably musical instruments and/or costumes, while that dance proper was brought to Japan in 612 by a Korean musician named Mimashi (Ortolani 1995: 29). A significant number of eighth-century *gigaku* masks – humanoid as well as animal – are preserved in the Shōsōin and the Tokyo National Museum. Like the masks featured on the Subashi *sarira*, the *gigaku* masks covered the entire head, had no movable parts, and, particularly those associated with the dance of the "Drunken Barbarian King" (Suiko-ō), feature the long noses of the Hu western barbarians (Ortolani 1995: 34; see Section 3, p. 32, and Figure 2). The *somakusa* was also an actual *bugaku* dance piece (still part of the Japanese court music repertoire today) originally played on the shaku-hachi flute; according to a legend, at the sound of the smooth melody the mountain god came out and began to dance, and it was on the basis of this dance that some court musician created the choreography of the court dance (Linder 2012: 225–27).

At the other extremity of the Asian continent, the *samāğa* was a masquerade of possibly Central Asian provenance and performed at the Abbasid courts in the ninth century (Borroni 2019). As Borroni noted, in the earliest-known description *samāğa* is linked to the water-splashing custom of the Nawrūz of celebrations of 834, while later descriptions continue the association with the Nawrūz and specify the presence of (animal) masks – at times extremely pricey – and the gracefulness of the line dance (Boronni 2019: 294 and 297). Moreover, the term *farāğina*, encountered in several sources with respect to either dancers or their masks, links the performances at the Abbasid court to Farghāna valley in Sogdiana (southeastern corner of present-day Uzbekistan), which, by all intents and purposes seems to have been the central node in the diffusion of *sumozhe/samāğa* from Central Asia to Kucha, China, Japan, and Iraq (Boronni 2019: 298).

If indeed the depictions on the drum of the Subashi *sarira* is that of a Kuchean procession of dancing and music-making participants in the Kuchean version of the *sumozhe* festival, that would render this artifact as one of the rare visual witnesses to the sights and sounds of one of the celebrations and dances with the most complex cultural history in Eurasia.

4.3 Tocharian Music Vocabulary

If Chinese texts and Kuchean music-iconographic sources have so far provided the bulk of the information pertaining to the musical life in the kingdom, the body of manuscript fragments in Tocharian has only recently emerged as a possible resource in the study of Kuchean musical practices (Currie in press).[20] The Kuchean music vocabulary reflects complex lexical and semantic intersections, resulting from the multilingual situation in the Tarim Basin in general, and Kucha in particular, during the first millennium CE. Not only have manuscripts in more than half a dozen languages and several different scripts been recovered in Kucha by archaeologists – including more than 10,000 Tocharian A and B fragments dating largely from the sixth to the eighth century – but also "the spatial closeness and the intense interaction of speech communities with many bi- or multilingual speakers produced contact phenomena and resulted in language change visible on all levels in the different codes" (Schaefer 2010, 450). One example encapsulating the intersection of language and music conceptualization can be found in a passage from the Tocharian Buddhist drama *Maitreyasamiti-Nāṭaka*:

> "puk / *swārantwaṃ* puk *kaṃsaṃ* puk / *murcchäntwaṃ* ṣāñ kalpoṣ poñśä / pu[k w]ä"
> ["in all sounds, in all melodies [and] in all modulations, all have obtained skill in every way"].[21]

The almost casual use in the Tocharian text of the Sanskrit loan terms *svara* (sound, pitch) and *mūrcchanā* (scale) is strong evidence for a link forged between Indian conceptualizations of musical space based on a system of pitches and related scales and the local concept of "melody," rendered by the Tocharian term *kaṃ*, all woven into a seamless poetic expression. Like the case of Sujiva's modal terminology, this and other such similar cases of the admixture of Sanskrit and Tocharian music terminology suggest that at least some Kuchean music conceptualizations were contingent upon Indian practices. This multilingual predisposition is absent, however, in the case of organological nomenclature. When we look at the entirety of what can reasonably be assumed are instrument names in the Tocharian corpus in the CEToM Project at the University of Vienna (Table 3), Sanskrit/Prakrit loanwords are mostly intriguingly absent even in those cases where they would name instruments clearly introduced into Kucha directly from the Indian subcontinent (with the exception of *paṭak*).

The coexistence of categorically distinct lexicons – largely Tocharian organological nomenclature on the one hand, and a fully integrated Sanskrit and Tocharian music-theoretical vocabulary on the other – coupled with a music instrumentarium and customs of diverse cultural provenances, stands witness to an entangled world of objects, terms, conceptualizations, and practices, all made manifest in the musician Sujiva, his Kuchean musical lineage, his *hu-pipa*, and his account of the "Western modes." The iconographic record and musical lexicon current in Kucha in

---

[20] Indispensable for such studies is the *Comprehensive Edition of Tocharian Manuscripts* (CEToM) Project at the University of Vienna: www.univie.ac.at/tocharian/.

[21] Emphasis added.

Table 3 Tocharian organological terminology

Type	Toch A	Toch B	English equivalent	Sanskrit/Pāli equivalent
Wind		*ploriyo*	flute/wind instrument (pl. musicians)	
String	*tsärk*	*śarka*	lute/string instrument	
Percussion	*karel (?)*	*kerū**	drum (kettle?)	(Skt. *dundubhi*)
		paṭak	drum (barrel?)	(Pāli *paṭaha*)
	kāltaṅk		drum	(Skt. *dundubhi*)
	kumpäc		drum	(Skt. *dundubhi*)
Unknown	*kispar wic*	*kera**		

the second part of the first millennium CE, together with the contemporaneous Chinese textual witnesses, point to a mature, organic, and cosmopolitan musical culture of intricately interwoven and synthesized Eurasian strands. It is a singularly complex case of musical cosmopolitanism, of music synergies that distinguish Kucha as an exceptional node within the vast Eurasian network of cultural exchanges.

5 Tracking the *Qopuz*: From Qocho to Herat

The Turkic term *qopuz* (Clauson 1972: 588–89; Doerfer 1967: 535–37), found in several orthographic variants, denotes a rather large and heterogenous range of instruments – mostly string instruments but also jaw harps and winds – which originally inhabited the Eurasian steppes, and had by the fourteenth century spread from the Tianshan to the Carpathians. By that time, instruments with some variant of this name were mentioned in sources as far west as the German lands, such as Heinrich von Neustadt's *Von Gottes Zukunft* (c. 1300): "Die kobus mit der luten / Damburen mit den bucken" (von Neustadt 1906: 400–1). Under this name and its derivations, all across Eurasia from medieval times until modern times, one can enumerate a variety of string instruments such as: two string-fiddles, including the Kazakh *qobyz* or *qyl-qobyz* and the Karakalpak *qobuz/qobiz*; short-neck lutes including the Ukrainian *kobza,* Hungarian *koboz,* and Romanian/Moldovan *cobza*; and long-necked lutes (with skin-covered sound-boards) including the older Kyrgyz *komuz,* and the Azeri and Ottoman *qopuz*. From the earliest-known written records – where the term most likely references a type of lute – to archaeological finds, funerary monuments, oral poetry, and tavern music, the *qopuz* was emblematic of the Turkic stratum of steppe music-cultures. Like many other musical instruments in motion through the Eurasian expanses, the *qopuz'* history was marked by dynamic encounters, translations, adaptations, and accommodations, from which emerge the *sine qua non* conceptual paradigms that accounts for both the terminological stability and the changes in instrument morphology, social function, and cultural meaning that define the worlds of the *qopuz*.

5.1 The Kingdom of Qocho

The Kharakanid scholar and lexicographer of the eleventh century, Maḥmūd al-Kāšġarī, seems to have come originally from Barsgan on the southern shores of the Issyk-Köl (in present-day Kyrgyzstan), in the region known as Semirechye or Yeti-su, "the land of the seven rivers." After having traveled extensively in many Turkic lands, he journeyed to Baghdad where he compiled his monumental *Dīwān lughāt al-turk* ("Compendium of the Languages of the Turks," 1075–94), the first comprehensive dictionary of Turkic dialects. The linguistic material he provides in this dictionary with reference to Turkic musical instruments and practices is indeed invaluable; moreover, since it is by and large a comparison-oriented explanatory dictionary, the Arabo-Persian organology he used as reference allows us to understand better the nature of the Turkic subjects. Al-Kāšġarī mentions the *qopuz* many times in different lexical or performative contexts, consistently equating the instrument – which according to him can be played by either male or female musicians – with the Arabic *'ūd*, *mazahir*, or *kiran* and, at times, comparing its sound (possibly in the Azeri version) to that of the Persian *barbat* (al-Kāšġarī 1982: II 72, 130, 238).

Its relevance notwithstanding, al-Kāšġarī's *Dīwān* is not the earliest source to mention our instrument. That distinction resides with a couple of manuscripts from the tenth or eleventh century, compiled in the Uighur kingdom of Qocho and found in Turfan and Dunhuang by German and French expeditions at the beginning of the twentieth century. The Qocho kingdom had its origins in the mid-ninth-century events in Mongolia that opened the gate toward the gradual Turkicization of a greater part of Inner Asia. The process was set in motion in 840 when the Kyrgyz, a Turkic people who lived along the upper Yenisei in the present-day republic of Tuva, overthrew the Uighur Khaganate of Mongolia. Some of the fleeing Uighurs settled in the eastern part of the Tianshan where they founded the kingdom of Qocho which lasted until the middle of the thirteenth century, and in the late tenth century began a gradual conversion from Manichaeism to Buddhism. The Uighur elites patronized Buddhism, Manichaeism, and East Syriac Christianity, as witnessed by the textual and artistic vestiges discovered in the Turfan region, as well as by the ruins of palaces and religious establishments in various locales, particularly in the area of

Qocho, the summer capital of the kingdom. The local populations combined Iranian, Tocharian, Sogdian, possibly Indian, and – particularly in Qocho – Chinese elements together with the Uighur. Linguistically and culturally, therefore, the kingdom preserved the penchant for cultural cosmopolitanism that had characterized the area prior to its foundation, while adding a further Turkic layer.

It is this multilingual, multireligious, and multiethnic environment that provides us with some of the earliest evidence of organological nomenclature circulating in the kingdom: both Old Uighur terminology – such as *yir* (song), *nay* (pipe or flute), *tsuitsi* (possibly a double-reed instrument), *tig* (flute), *küvrüg* (drum), and *čımkuylug yir* (lit. "mouth organ and song") – and Chinese loanwords such as *čüŋ* (bell; equiv. Ch. *zhong* 鐘), *labay* (conch shell, equiv. Ch. *luo-bei* 螺貝). An instrument by the name of *qopuz* is mentioned in a couple of texts, in contexts that give us a sense of its possible positioning in the musical world of the kingdom. One passage from a Uighur-Manichean wedding blessing from Turfan – written in Syriac script characteristic to the tenth-to-twelfth century – speaks of the bride and groom's relatives in musical terms: "As the *qopuz* [long-necked lute] and the *kišak* [*gījak*; spike fiddle] play together, as the *čïmquq* [finger cymbals? mouth organ?] and the *čïngïrčaq* [cymbals?] sound together, may their relatives by marriage work together, and may there be eating, drinking, and rejoicing!" (Dickens 2016: 111–12; modified). It is possible that the mention of two instruments with Turkic names – the *gījak* and the *qopuz* – in a Manichean text representative of the pre-Buddhist Uighur stratum may not be coincidental. Yet, an even earlier source exists: the Uighur version of the Buddhist story of Kalyāṇaṃkara and Pāpaṃkara found in a manuscript from Mogao Cave 17 in Dunhuang written in a tenth-century Uighur script (Pelliot 1914; Hamilton 1971). Significant for our purposes here is the point in the story when prince Ädgü-ökli (Kalyāṇaṃkara), declaring himself a mendicant, requests that he be given a *qoŋkau* with which he would accompany his singing; once given the *qoŋkau*, the prince sits himself in the center of the town surrounded by a large crowd, where he begins to skillfully play his instrument, which this time is identified by the term *qopuz (kopuz)*.

The *qoŋkau* Ädgü-ökli plays in this story most certainly was the Chinese angular harp, the *konghou*. While *qoŋkau* is a Chinese loan word referencing a harp, *qopuz* is the Turkic term that, as repeatedly attested by al-Kāšġarī in his dictionary, references a lute. The substitution of *konghou* with *qopuz* mid-story is somewhat puzzling. The process of substitution may in part depend on the lexical and organological flexibility permitted by the transmission of the Buddhist story in many versions and languages; the Chinese version, for example, has the prince playing not the *konghou* harp as it may be expected, but a zither, the *zheng* (Chavannes 1914: 491). This flexibility may also point to

a kind of implicit bi-musicality (organological as well as terminological) pecu-
liar to the Uighur scribe and its audience. This Buddhist story has the blind good
prince (Ädgü-ökli in our version) become a mendicant who takes up singing and
playing for a living. In Sanskrit/Prakrit Buddhist literature, the instrument at the
center of such an enterprise is customarily a *vīṇa* (arched harp), which is
consistently translated in Chinese as *konghou* (angular harp); the Uighur version thus preserves this text-oriented organological choice. The switch away
from the *qoŋkau/konghou* occurs at the point when the prince begins to perform
in the center of the town and enthralls the crowd of people day after day. It may
be an accidental scribal switch or, more likely, a deliberate one, since it aligns
well with the fact that it was indeed a musician playing the *qopuz* who
commonly was at the center of such early Turkic performance spaces and
contexts.

This entanglement of terms, objects, and text and performing traditions that
these examples bring to light maps quite well onto the religious and linguistic
diversity that defined the everyday life in the kingdom. It also sheds light on
a bi-musical world of co-existing Chinese and Turkic instruments, ensembles,
and probably practices that nevertheless indexed distinct sociocultural
domains. There is indeed significant evidence, textual as well as visual, that
the *qoŋkau/konghou* and other Chinese musical instruments were a familiar
occurrence in the Uighur kingdom, where they seem to have inhabited sacred
and courtly milieus. For example, Wang Yande 王延德 (939–1006), the Song
envoy who visited Qocho in the 980s, writes in his account of the visit that
"[t]heir music is largely played on the pipa and harp [*konghou*]" (Millward
2007: 48). The stake inscription from 1008 commissioned by a local high-
ranking couple mentions, among others, the harpist (*kuŋkawčı*) Boguncu who
provided the music for the consecrations of the newly founded Buddhist
monastery (Wilkens 2015: 202). Furthermore, the Chinese *konghou* is represented in some of the surviving murals of the area, such as the ruins of the
palace east of Qocho; here, the musicians – all Uighur dignitaries who are
indexed as such by the trident-shaped head-ornament they wear (Esin 1970:
93–94) – play an array of Chinese musical instruments including the *pipa* and
the *konghou* (Figure 11).

Even though elite instrumental contexts featuring Chinese lutes and harps
dominate the iconographical record, there is at least one possible depiction in
Uighur art of a vernacular instrument consistent with the Turkic *qopuz*. A ninth-
century Buddhist temple banner from Yar-khoto (Turfan; Berlin, Museum für
Indische Kunst MIK III 6302) depicts Hāritī, the tutelary goddess of children,
nursing a baby at her bosom while surrounded by eight small children at play; some
of the children are playing ball, one is carrying a bowl of melon slices, and another

Figure 11 Musical ensemble. Qocho, Khan's Palace. Source: Grünwedel 1912, *Altbuddhistische Kultstätten in Chinesisch-Turkistan*, vol. 1, p. 333, fig. 664.

is playing a string instrument (Figure 12). The instrument is a lute carved out from a single block, with a relatively long neck, a perfectly round belly covered with leather, and the rest of the body slightly barbed; it has four strings with the pegs aligned on one single side and the neck of the instrument slightly bent (Figure 13). Could the instrument Hārītī's child plucks be identified as a *qopuz*?

Iconographic and textual evidence are often difficult to align in the identification of an instrument, and, to make things even more difficult, the *qopuz* historically belongs to a larger family of instruments known from textual sources of West and Inner Asia, which are all leather-bellied, plucked lutes that include the *shidurghū, rubāb, qūpūz-e rumī, qūpūz-e ozan, and rūdkhānī.* The one possible alternative name for Hārītī's child's instrument is the *shidurghū* (Doerfer 1967: 365), the classical form of the modern Mongolian *shudraga/shidurgu,* a three-stringed, long-necked lute with a skin-covered sound-chest (Tsuge 2019: 350).

The Timurid music theorist Abd al-Qādir al-Marāghī b. Ghaybī (d. 1435) describes the *shidurghū* of his era thus: "*Shidurghū* is played mostly by the people of *Khatā'ī.* Four strings are mounted on this instrument. [The sound-chest of this lute] is long, and half of its surface is covered with skin" (Tsuge 2019: 348). Al-Marāghī links this instrument with the 'people of *Khatā'ī*', referring to the Khitans who formed the Liao dynasty in northern China from 907 to 1125; this firmly places the *shidurghū*, like the *qopuz*, in the world of

Figure 12 Hāritī nursing a baby at her bosom while surrounded by eight small
children at play. Buddhist temple banner from Yar-khoto, Turfan (ninth
century). Berlin MIK III 6302. Source: Le Coq 1913, *Chotscho*, [p. 41], pl. 40.

steppe lutes. Al-Marāghī also describes two types of *qopuz*: the *qopuz-e rumī*
(possibly the Anatolian version) that has five double strings and is carved out of
a piece of wood with skin stretched over its surface; and the [*qopuz-e*] *ozan* that
has three single strings and a longer bowl with skin stretched over half of its
surface (Picken 1975: 266). Granted, al-Marāghī's descriptions pertain to
a much more recent organological world than the documents in the Qocho
kingdom, yet among his skin-covered lutes, only the *shidurghū* has four strings,

Figure 13 Hāritī nursing a baby at her bosom while surrounded by eight small children at play (detail). Buddhist temple banner from Yar-khoto, Turfan (ninth century). Berlin MIK Ill 6302. Source: Le Coq 1913, *Chotscho*, [p. 41], pl. 40.

and thus would accord most closely with the instrument played by Hāritī's child. Remarkably, the lute played by the child has a striking parallel in the contemporary world: the *sugudu* 苏古篤 (etymologically probably related to our *shidurghū*), a rather unique four-string lute known also as *hubo* 胡撥 (term possibly related to *huobosi* 火撥思, the Chinese version of the *qopuz*) still extant in the musical traditions of the Naxi, an ethnic group at the foothills of the Himalayas (Northwest Yunnan and Southwest Sichuan Province in the PRC) (Rees 2000: 70–71).[22] The absence of any textual evidence for an instrument named *shidurghū* in the kingdom of Qocho may indeed cast some doubt upon such an identification, yet, allowing for wider morphological and terminological flexibility for the instruments in question, makes it quite conceivable that the instrument played by Hārītī's child could have been called a *qopuz*.

Textual and iconographical ambiguities such as these reflect the well-known terminological and to some extent morphological fluidity characterizing many early instruments across time and space. Along with the challenging intersections of geographies and histories involved, the limitations of extant visual and textual evidence present significant challenges in determining an accurate record of the early circulation networks of musical instruments in Eurasia. Possibly adding some pieces to our current puzzle is archeological data, both in terms of funerary inscriptions and in terms of actual instruments uncovered at archaeological sites across the steppes.

5.2 Between the Tianshan and the Altai

The Chinese pilgrim and Buddhist scholar, Xuanzang (602–64) provides us with one of the earliest accounts of music-making among the Western Turks. Leaving the Kucha kingdom in the northern Tarim Basin behind, Xuanzang followed one of the main routes used at the time by Western Turks in Central Asia to communicate with their Tarim Basin dependencies, crossing the Tianshan mountains by the Bedel pass to reach the shores of lake Issyk-Köl ("the warm lake"; present-day Kyrgyzstan). Shortly after, he met Tung Yabğu (r. 618/619?–630), the Great Khan of the Western Turks at Suyab (modern Ak Beshim, Kyrgyzstan), the principal capital of the Khaganate, and was the guest of honor at a banquet where the Great Khan

> was much elated and caused the envoys to be seated, then he ordered wine and music for himself and them and grape-syrup for the pilgrim. Hereupon all pledged each other and the filling and passing and draining of the winecups made a din and bustle, while the *mingled music of various instruments* [apparently indexing different types of music] rose loud: although the airs were the popular strains of foreigners, yet they pleased the senses and exhilarated the mental faculties.
>
> (Watters 1904: 74–75; emphasis added; see also Watters' commentary on
> the passage on pp. 88–89)

Xuanzang does not describe any specific instrument, sounds, or details of the performance, only that he found the foreign songs aesthetically pleasing to the

---

[22] www.robertharding.com/preview/657-483/naxi-orchestra-pracisting-black-dragon-pool-lijiang-yunnan/; see also, building a *sugudu* /www.youtube.com/watch?v=tC3OLYU-4Yg(6'54" ff.).

ear and invigorating to the mind. Help in providing some hints as to what kind of instruments might have participated in the merrymaking at the court of the Great Khan comes from the field of archaeology. Several musical instruments were recently uncovered during archaeological excavations of a complex of Turk burial mounds in Karabaka valley in the Altai (present-day eastern Kazakhstan) (Zhalmaganbetov, Samashev & Umitkaliev 2015).[23] The excavation uncovered three mounds dating from the seventh to the ninth century, which contain musical instruments. All three are structured around two burial pits: each has one pit with the remains of a horse, and another pit with the remains of an individual surrounded by military accoutrements (saber, quiver, arrow, helmet) and a musical instrument. The instruments in two of the mounds are clearly lutes carved from a single piece of wood, with long necks and sound-chests formerly covered with skin (around 63 cm and 70 cm in length, respectively); one has a boat-shaped sound-chest while the other a bowl-shaped one. The instrument in the third grave is poorly preserved, but the surviving headstock with four pegs and fingerboard suggests a type of plucked four-stringed lute (Zhalmaganbetov, Samashev & Umitkaliev 2015: 548–50). The fact that all three instruments seem to belong to the same family and are by and large contemporaneous with Xuanzang's pilgrimage is relevant, since it reinforces the link between the family of skin-bellied long-necked lutes and the Turkic musical world and renders such instruments as likely participants in the Great Khan's banquet at Suyab. However, to come across the name *qopuz* – tenuously linked to such instruments – we need to return south, to the area not far from where the Great Khan's banquet took place, and at the same time allow for a gap of several centuries.

The rich epigraphical corpus in Syriac script, consisting of more than 600 tombstone inscriptions from East Syriac cemeteries situated in the Chu Valley not far from lake Issyk-Köl, includes at least three inscriptions that refer to deceased individuals with musical abilities. Two of them (in the Syriac language) refer to the departed as having voices sounding like an instrument, in a rhetorical simile that could pertain to timbre, nuance, or sonic projection. The earlier inscription dates from 1315, "the year of the eclipse," and refers to Shliḥa, the renowned expositor and preacher whose voice elated like the sound of a trumpet (Chwolson 1886: 14, no. 8; Dickens 2016: 111). The inscription thus not only commemorates a member of the religious community but also marks the time of his death by a celestial phenomenon: the total solar eclipse perfectly visible from the Chu Valley on May 4, 1315 (Mahler 1887).

---

[23] For good photographs taken *in situ*, see www.thehistoryblog.com/archives/31836 and https://e-history.kz/en/news/show/8013/.

The second inscription commemorates Čakuš the priest, whose voice sounded like a harp and who died in 1339 (Chwolson 1897: 18, no. 69; Dickens 2016: 110), possibly at the time of the plague that began in the fourteenth century (Slavin 2019).

The third inscription is written completely in Turkic and, as in the other two instances, the date is given in two systems: the Seleucid system adopted by the East Syriac church and the Turkic calendar. It reads:

> (According to) the calculation of Alexander Khan it was one thousand six hundred twenty-three [1311/12 CE], it was the Turkic year of the Mouse. This is the grave of Mangu Tāš-tāy the *qopuz player* [*qopuzči*]. May he be remembered.
>
> (Chwolson 1897: 18, no. 69; Dickens 2016, 110; emphasis added)

This *qopuzči* with a Turkic name (according to Mark Dickens, the name Mangu Tāš-tāy is Turkic for "like an eternal stone"), who apparently received a Christian burial at the beginning of the fourteenth century in an East Syriac community in the vicinity of lake Issyk-Köl, represents a fascinating case of music-historical entanglements and multiple sociocultural layers, not only as an early reference to the instrument per se, the object of human agency, but also to the musician himself, the one who makes the instrument sound in the act of performance, the player of *qopuz*.

5.3 Desht-i Qipchaq

Both terms, *qopuz* and *qopuzči*, are found aplenty in a large number of late thirteenth- and early fourteenth-century sources, such as: in the poetry attributed to Yūnüs Emre, the wandering minstrel whose poetry composed in Old Anatolian (the precursor of Ottoman) was orally transmitted until the mid-fifteenth century (Peacock 2019: 158); in the older substratum of the Oghuz oral epic of Dede Korkut (a *qolča qopuz* player himself) (Reichl 1992: 43–55), dealing with the conflicts between the Oghuz, Pechenegs, and Cuman-Qïpčaqs (Curta 2019: 152–178); and in dictionaries and glossaries such as those contained in the late thirteenth-century *Codex Cumanicus* (Kuun 1981) and the later *Rasulid Hexaglot* (Golden 2000). Among the several entries that are music-related in the mid-fourteenth-century *Rasulid Hexaglot* – a six-language glossary compiled by or for the Rasulid king of Yemen al-Malek al-Afẓal al-ʿAbbās (r. 1363–77) – there is one pertaining to the Arabic ʿal-ṭunbûrî' (player of the *ṭunbûr*, long-necked lute), for which the glossary provides the following equivalents: 'muṭrib' (Pers.), 'qopuzči' (Türki), and 'quhurči' (Mong.) (Golden 2000: 306). The Persian 'muṭrib' aside (musician or minstrel, with no organological specificity), the other names refer to a musician as a player of a culturally specific string instrument clearly from the same family of long-necked lutes.

A different kind of conceptual equivalency appears in the much earlier *Codex Cumanicus*, more specifically in the portion that contains the late thirteenth-century Latin/Persian/Cuman-Qıpčaq glossary probably compiled by Italian merchants or Franciscan monks engaged in trade or missionary work in the region between the lower Volga and the Crimea (MacKenzie, n.d.). This is the region at the heart of *Desht-i Qıpčaq* – the Cuman-Qıpčaq confederation of mainly Turkic tribes that, between the tenth and the thirteenth century, occupied the territory of the belt of Eurasian forest-steppe from the Altai to the slopes of the Carpathians. In a section dedicated to musical vocabulary, the glossary introduces a set of interesting trilingual terminological parallels (e.g. *ca[n]tator/serot guenda/yrci*; *tronbe/nafir/burgular; caramella/surna/suruna*, etc.) among which we encounter *sonator/mutrub/cobuxci* (Kuun 1981: 103–4). In the Latin-dominated world of our European compilers in Crimea – imperfectly as they may have represented Cuman-Qıpčaq organological meanings – the *cobuxci* (lit. *qopuz* player) stands metonymically for a generic instrumentalist comparable to the Latin *sonator* (instrument player) and the Persian *muṭrib* (musician, entertainer). Without being assigned a specific instrumental counterpart, our Crimean *qopuzči* may very well be playing any kind of plucked or bowed lute.

In 1983–85, archaeologists excavated the thirteenth-century burial mound of such a *qopuzči* just north of Crimea, near the village of Kirove (Kherson Oblast, present-day Ukraine). The grave goods accompanying the deceased male included a bow with arrows and a quiver and a three-stringed spoon-shaped lute carved from a single piece of wood, together with what archaeologists identified as a playing bow. The sound-chest of the lute is long and narrow (equal in length to what is believed to be the bow of the instrument) with resonating sound holes and a small bridge, and was originally probably covered with skin. Three grooves on the fingerboard indicate the existence of frets; three holes drilled in the head of the fingerboard would have accommodated three pegs (Gershkovich 2011: 85–86; figs. 5–7).

An instrument almost identical in proportion and observable morphology – yet lacking the bow – was carved at the feet of a Cuman-Qıpčaq warrior-statue, today housed in the Simferopol Museum (Figure 14). Such statues also have a funerary symbolism attached to them. We know from the oldest extant Turkic writings – for example, the Orkhon inscriptions from the mid-eighth century – that figures such as this were called *balbals* and that they were erected by the Turks in memory of the dead, possibly representing the deceased individuals

Figure 14 Cuman-Qıpčaq warrior-statue with musical instrument carved at its feet (left). Simferopol Museum, Crimea, Ukraine. Source: Veselovskiy 1915, Table 6.

themselves (Barthold & Rogers 1970: 196–97). We also know from William of Rubruck's mid-thirteenth-century account that such statues were erected by the nomadic inhabitants of the South Russian steppes to commemorate their dead: "The Comans raise a great tumulus over the dead, and set up a statue to him, its face to the east, and holding a cup in its hand at the height of the navel" (William of Rubruck 1990: 95). It is, therefore, very likely that the Simferopol *balbal*, with its carved lute at the feet of the human figure, is a monument that commemorates a *qopuzči*. In the case of the Cuman-Qıpčaqs, therefore, terminology, archaeology, and iconography seem indeed to intersect in a most fortunate manner.

Archaeologists typically refer to all the lutes they excavated at sites scattered across the steppes, from the Altai mountains to Crimea and beyond, with a version of the term *qopuz*; moreover, they all tend to view them all as ancestors of whichever particular version of the instrument exists in the present-day musical traditions of their respective modern nation-states. Such historical links should be regarded with skepticism, though. The very few comparative archaeological, iconographic, and textual samples, dispersed over an enormous geographical area and many centuries, do not allow for the construction of a historical narrative rigorous enough to suggest continuities with modern practices. Moreover, casually linking the "medieval" and the "modern" in such a manner disregards the host of additional cultural encounters and exchanges that are known to have occurred in the intervening time, encounters that helped diversify, possibly standardize, and at times drastically transform the morphology and performance practices associated with many musical instruments.

That the *qopuz*'s shape and performance technique would have not necessarily remained exactly the same across diverse musical geographies and over almost half a millennium – from the Uighur kingdom of Qocho, to the Eastern Syrian communities of the Chu valley near lake Issyk-Köl, to the Crimean Cuman-Qıpčaqs – seems a sound conjecture, one that would also explain the difficulties encountered in the process of reading the extant evidence. Amid these variables, though, there is at least one apparent constant. In many of these communities, whenever we encounter the *qopuz* – be that as a term or as an object – it was apparently associated with rites of passage: as a participant in the symbolic union of a wedding in the Uighur-Manichean blessing, and as a companion to its player in the Turkic steppe burial customs. Particularly intriguing in the latter case is the ubiquitous coexistence of musical instruments, sabers, and bows and arrows in each of the burial sites mentioned here, as well as some evidence of skull trephination, which might have been performed to facilitate states of altered consciousness characteristic to shamanistic practices. This potential bardic-shamanistic entanglement in the early history of the early instrument and its practices is quite fascinating and resonates with the lore surrounding modern practices in Central Asia, yet more evidence is needed to support such a hypothesis. Thus far, archaeological and textual documentation attest to the fact that such early lutes with a skin-covered belly had long been extant in the Turkic world and at times seem to have been associated with individual musicians, minstrels who came to carry the name of their instrument or whose instrument accompanied them in the afterlife. What is also undeniable, is that by the time of the last Cuman-Qıpčaq *balbals* in late thirteenth century, the *qopuz* had already gone beyond the boundaries of the steppe cultures, and that the social contexts surrounding its presence in the 'new' host-cultures were expanding rapidly.

5.4 Timurid Taverns

In the fourteenth century, the *qopuz* was already known in China under the name *huobusi* [火撥思] and had been integrated in the grand orchestra at the Yuan court (Lam 1994: 179, n. 33) together with one other instrument of "western" provenance, the Ilkhanid organ (see Section 6.5). The *History of Yuan* 元史 (*Yuanshi*) describes the *huobusi* in these terms: "*Huobusi* is built like a pipa. The neck is straight, and without frets. The lute has a small sound-chest, the round face of which resembles an ancient wine vessel and is covered with skin. Four strings are mounted over a single bridge" (Tsuge 2019: 350). A comparison with its contemporaneous West Asian relatives as described by al-Marāghī (see pp. 53–54) is instructive. The Chinese *huobusi* and al-Marāghī's two versions of the *qopuz* all have different numbers of strings but they share one important feature: the skin-covered belly. It is a feature held in common with the instruments excavated at both the Altai and the Crimean sites, some of which had three strings, just like the al-Marāghī *qopuz* of the Oghuz minstrels.

   In the fifteenth century, with the establishment of courtly Timurid culture in Herat and the growing prestige of Chagatai (Turkic) literature, the *qopuz*, together with several other Turkic instruments, gradually became integrated (literarily and musically) into the larger, cosmopolitan Arabo-Persian-Mongol instrumentarium, particularly in the context of urban entertainment. For example, ʿAlī Shīr Nawāʾī (d. 1501), the great Timurid poet, scholar, and fierce supporter and proponent of Chagatai as a language superior to Persian, writes in his *Maḥbūb al-qulūb* ("The Beloved of Hearts") that:

> In the drinking-place (*maykhāna*), even for the man who abstains from alcohol, well, the voice of the *nay* (flute) will make him drink . . . with its attractive song. Even if a man avoids the call of wine, when the *gījak* (spike fiddle) lamentingly implores him to drink, when the *tanbur* (long-necked lute) incites him to shameless-ness with its noise, when the *chang* (harp) dries up his throat with its plaints and by its very language the 'ud (short-necked lute) again calls on him to drink; while the *rabāb* (lute) prostrates itself and begs him to drink and the *qopuz* seizes his ears and fills them with music that draws him towards pleasure.
>
> (Cited in Papas 2019: 35; slightly modified)

The *qopuz*, together with its old partner in the Uighur-Manichean wedding blessing, the *gījak,* are here the two Turkic instruments that, together with a flute (*nay*), the harp (*chang*), and several lutes (*tanbur, 'ud,* and *rabāb*), all part of the Arabo-Persian instrumentarium, participate in the cosmopolitan musical environment of a late fifteenth-century tavern in Herat, where with their sound they entice the hearers to the pleasure of drinking. The anthropomorphized sounds of the instruments – the direct approach of the *nay, 'ud,* and *chang,* which alternates with the imploring, inciting, and begging tones of the *gījak, tanbur,* and *rabāb* – steer the tavern guest toward the threshold of an almost mystical experience induced by the sound of the *qopuz.* Clearly, when it comes to sonic persuasion, the *qopuz* reigns.

Another fictional tavern of the early fifteenth century is the scene for the rather amusing *Sāzlar munāẓarasi* ("Dispute of String Instruments"), also written in Chagatai Turkic idiom by the otherwise unknown poet Ahmadī (Bodrogligeti 1987). Here, the *tanbura* (long-necked lute) mocks and belittles a host of other instruments that are hanging around the tavern, each loosely associated with a specific class of performers or audiences: the Arabo-Persian *'ud* (lute), the king of the instruments; the *chang* (harp), the king's companion; the *yātūghān* (the Mongol half-tube zither) associated with the warrior class; the *rabāb* (bowed-string instrument) of the Sufi dervishes; the *kingira* (stick-zither related to the *kendrā* of Rajasthan) of the ascetics; and our two old Turkic acquaintances, the *qopuz* and the *gījak,* the instruments of the princes and of the itinerant story-tellers (Lawergren, Neubauer & Kadyrov 2000: 606). Ahmadī's poem can be seen as yet another allegorical depiction of the colorful and cosmopolitan music scene of the Timurid era beyond the courtly environment. It represents much more than that, though, since it can be read as an projection of the systemic hybridity of Timurid society on to a similarly hybrid yet carefully configured hierarchy of musical instruments. Even though this hierarchy upholds Persian-Arabic dominance and prestige, it nevertheless accounts for the musical legacy of the self-perceived Central Asian "newcomers," the Turks, and their preceding Mongol brethren. In sum, it can be read as a Chagatai literary equivalent of the Timurid polity at the center of which reside the *qopuz* and the *gījak.*

The large variety of musical instruments encountered in the Timurid taverns is matched only by the cosmopolitanism of the Timurid courtly musical practices, as captured in one of the most fascinating accounts of the intense musical diversity that permeated the extensive celebrations held in Samarkand in the fall of 1404 to mark the weddings of several of Timur's sons. The passage is found with some slight differences in the works of two Timurid historians: Sharaf al-Dīn 'Alī Yazdī (d. 1454) (Sultanova 2011: 5) and Ḥāfiẓ-i Abrū (d. 1430). According to Ḥāfiẓ-i Abrū, sweet-voiced singers played instruments and sang songs following the way (*tariqa*) of the Persians, the system (*tartīb*) of the (unspecified) Persianate peoples (*'ağam*), the rules (*qaida*) of the Arabs, the custom *(yosun)* of the Turk, the melodies (*ayālğū*) of the Mongols, the rules (*rasm*) of the Chinese, and the custom (*siyaqi*) of the Altai people (Tauer 1934: 446; Doerfer 1967: 195). What does this account actually tell us? It tells us that in the highly eclectic musical surroundings of Timurid festivities, musicians of unspecified ethnolinguistic appurtenance brought together, in the act of performance, songs following musical rules, systems, laws, and customs from across Eurasia. What the text does not tell us, however, are any specifics. In other words, were there different ensembles, each one of them dwelling on a culturally identifiable repertoire, as in the Tang court? Or were the musicians in fact participating in the creation of multicultural sonic syntheses that lent themselves to skillful parsing by the analytically keen ethnographic eye of our historians? And, most importantly, what exactly were the "way of the Persians" and "the rules of the Arabs," "the custom of the Turks" or the "melodies of the Mongols"? In many ways, any attempt to reimagine these rules and customs is most likely as hopeless as trying to bring back to life the mystical song of the *qopuz* enticing guests to drinking in the Herat taverns.

From the steppes of the Altai to the taverns of Herat, from Uighur-Manichean wedding symbolism to funeral traditions in seemingly bardic and/or shamanistic contexts, from the largely oral epics of the nomadic Oghuz and Cuman-Qıpčaqs to the Persianate tropes of Chagatai literature, the complex early history of skin-bellied lutes in premodern Eurasia remains sparsely documented and – as of yet – inadequately researched. Associated from very early on with steppe musical cultures, the Turkic term *qopuz* generically denoted the concept of 'musical instrument', and particularly indexed the skin-bellied lute. Throughout its history and in all its variants, the *qopuz* was an organological marker for cultures in the Turkic linguistic world. Most, if not all, textual references come from sources in Turkic languages, from the Uighur documents mentioned earlier to the innumerable occurrences in Anatolian Turkic and Chagatai writings of the fourteenth and later centuries. A more in-depth consideration than possible here of textual, archeological, and iconographical evidence linked to the circulation of the *qopuz* in the Eurasian spaces may well describe what seems to be an exceptional case, where the instrument and its people journey together.

6 Sound-Making Mechanical Marvels

6.1 Automata

Complex automata, mechanical objects that are self-operating after having been activated, were designed and perfected in multicultural Hellenistic Alexandria by engineers who combined artistic talent and technical prowess, chief among whom stood Ctesibios of Alexandria (fl. c. 270 BCE), Philon of Byzantium (fl. c. 200 BCE), and Heron of Alexandria (c. 10–70 CE). They populated their writings with descriptions of numerous automata, both mobile and stationary, both silent and sonorous: water clocks, pneumatic and hydraulic organs, containers that could adjust the flow of different liquids, automatically opening temple doors accompanied by the sound of a trumpet, fountains or containers of water equipped with singing birds or other sound figures, and others. Moreover, as Adrienne Mayor has recently shown, "many of the self-moving devices and automata described in the mythical traditions of Greece and Rome – and in comparable lore of ancient India and China – . . . were thought of as manufactured products of technology, designed and constructed from scratch using the same materials and methods that human artisans used to make tools, artworks, buildings, and statues" (Mayor 2018: 2). Whether material or mythical, automata of the medieval world have only more recently become the focus of literary and art historical scholarship, in addition to that of history of science and technology (e.g. S. Farmer 2013; Deluz 2017; Ambrosetti 2019; and esp. Truitt 2015). It is regrettable, though, that sound automata have also so far received far greater attention as examples of technology and science of mechanics than as devices participating in sonic landscapes. Inasmuch as they create sound mechanically, they merit consideration as musical instruments of sorts and can carry culture-specific musical meanings and values. In light of the conceptual distinction, common since antiquity, between useful devices and those designed to elicit delight and wonder, it is clear that "autophonic" devices, even more than the purely kinetic ones, shatter the principle of practical utility. While lacking an evident pragmatic purpose, automated sound certainly contributed nonetheless to arousing amazement, astonishment, pleasure, and (sometimes) fear. At the same time, from late antiquity onward, sounding automata came to be part of complex systems, symbolically manifesting power in order to enact the acceptance or at least the acknowledgement of that power, be that in the context of direct encounters or gift exchange (Dessì 2010). Wonder, delight, leisure, pleasure, ingenuity, and projection of power have all been constant aspirations not only in Mediterranean antiquity, but also in the Eurasian expanses, where long-held fascination with musical automata, whether they were actually built or only imagined, featured notably in various imperial soundscapes spanning from Chang'an to Dhara-nagara and Byzantium, from Baghdad to Karakorum.

6.2 Thrones, Birds, and Fountains

The Byzantine 'Throne of Solomon', reportedly constructed by the engineer Leo the Mathematician (790–c. 869), is undoubtedly the best-known kinetic and

sonic set of mechanical devices that embodied imperial might and power by
means of both its construction and its very specific function in the context of
courtly rituals (Brett 1954). This complex set of automata, which included
roaring lions as well as singing birds on a tree, together with organs that flanked
the throne itself, was set in motion in order to strike foreign legates with awe
when they visited the emperor in the Magnaura, the ceremonial hall in the great
palace of Constantinople. Two detailed tenth-century accounts concur in their
general descriptions.

Liutprand of Cremona (c. 920–72), as a legate of Berengar II of Italy,
recounts his reception in 949 CE by the Byzantine Emperor Constantine VII
Porphyrogenitos (905–59 CE) in a narrative style that brings to life his first
encounter with the awe-inspiring mechanical devices and the multisensorial
display of imperial power at the Byzantine court:

> In front of the Emperor's throne was set up a *tree of gilded bronze, its
> branches filled with birds, likewise made of bronze gilded over, and these
> emitted cries appropriate to their different species.* Now the Emperor's throne
> was made in such a cunning manner that at one moment it was down on the
> ground, while at another it rose higher and was seen to be up in the air. This
> throne was of immense size and was, as it were, guarded by lions, made either
> of bronze or wood covered with gold, which struck the ground with their tails
> and roared with open mouth and quivering tongue . . . As I came up, *the lions
> began to roar and the birds to twitter, each according to its kind.* . . . I lifted
> my head and behold! The man whom I had just seen sitting at a moderate
> height from the ground had now changed his vestments and was sitting as
> high as the ceiling of the hall court.
>
> (Cited in Mango 1997: 209–10; emphasis added)

The auditory magnificence of the scene resides in the sounds of the gilded tree
automaton filled with mechanical birds emitting "cries appropriate to their
different species" and of the similarly gilded roaring mechanical lions guarding
the immense imperial throne. All this augments, and in turn is augmented by, the
kinetic dimension, the majestic ascent of the throne that brings the Emperor
close to the level of the ceiling.

A contemporaneous Byzantine source, *De cerimoniis aulae Byzantinae*
(c. 959), provides a comparable description of the reception of the foreign
delegations at the Magnaura. Since it is an insider narrative, so to speak, the
account lacks the overwhelming awe and sense of astonishment, concentrat-
ing on the details of the ritual rather than on its impact on the onlooker. In
this careful coordination of sound and motion within the ritual choreography, the presence or absence of the sounds produced by birds and lions not
only marks the entrance and the exit of the legates, but also – with the

emperor silent throughout – they function as his "voice"; they "speak" in his stead:

> Whilst the Logothete asks the customary questions of the legate, *the lions begin to roar and the birds, those on the throne as well as those in the trees, begin to sing harmoniously*; and the animals on the throne rise from their places on the steps. .... after a short *time the organs cease, and the lions are silent, the birds stop singing* and the animals on the throne resume their usual places. .... and as he [the legate] goes out *the organs sound, and the lions and the birds all utter their own voices*, and all the animals rise from their places on the steps. And when the foreigner goes out through the curtain, *the organs and the birds cease*, and the animals resume their usual places.
>
> (*De cerimoniis* II, 15; tr. Featherstone 2007: 83–84)

The Byzantine throne may very well have been intended to engage in a dialogue or even contest of symbolic power with Abbasid sovereigns and their matching language of cultural representation. Byzantine dignitaries themselves described a strikingly similar mechanical tree, with artificial singing birds perched on its silver and gold branches, during a mission to the Abbasid court in 917. Caliph al-Muqtadir (908–32 CE/296–320 AH) gave the embassy a tour of the Dar al-Khilafa (Abode of the Caliphate) palace in Baghdad, with a stop to see its central piece, the sounding automaton in the Dar al-Shajarah (Hall of the Tree). Here, at the center of a round pond, stood a silver tree with gold and silver singing birds perched on its eighteen moving branches with enameled leaves swaying in the wind:

> When the two envoys entered, they kissed the ground, gave their greeting, and stopped at the place indicated by Nasr the chamberlain. Al-Muqtadir gave out the order for the opening of the cupola (*qubbah*) and the working of the tree, which came out of the ground by means of various mechanical devices until it filled the cupola. The fountains, gushing forth rose water and musk, were turned on, and the figurines (*tamathil*) of birds perching on the tree chirped. (Qaddūmī 1996: 154)

The rising of the tree from the ground and the accompanying chirping of the birds – motion and sound activated at the will of the ruler just as in the case of the Byzantine throne – work hand in hand to project the intended sense of astonishment in the face of vast riches and power. Granted, the Byzantines and Abbasids shared a taste for such automata and their respective technologies were based on the same principles devised by engineers of late antiquity. The presence in the Byzantine and Abbasid realms of mechanical trees with singing birds perched on their branches, highlights, however, the complex relationship that existed between the two cultures in terms of exchange, influence, and common legacies. It may very well be that mechanical designs of sound-making objects developed both in competition and exchange between Constantinople and Baghdad, at a time when ideas and technologies moved across geographical and cultural spaces relatively freely.

Related technologies appear to have been mastered and employed in the construction of an altogether different yet similarly awe-inspiring kind of pleasure object, the fountain observed at the court of Möngke Khan (r. 1251–59) in Karakorum in spring 1254. Described by the Franciscan traveler William of Rubruck and attributed to Guillaume Boucher – a Parisian goldsmith captured by the Mongols at Belgrade in 1242 and taken to Karakorum – the "magic fountain" of the Mongol took the shape of a great silver tree with four silver lions at its roots, each spouting through a conduit a different beverage: grape wine, mare's milk, honey mead, and rice mead. On top of the fountain, Boucher placed an angel holding a trumpet, and underneath the tree he built a vault in which a man could hide. In a rare and rather amusing instance of failed first-choice technology, Boucher "made bellows, but they did not give enough wind"; therefore, insofar as the sound component was concerned, "when drink is required, the head butler calls to the angel to sound the trumpet. ... [T]he man concealed in the cavity then blows strongly on the pipe that leads to the angel, the angel puts the trumpet to its mouth, and the trumpet gives out a very loud blast" (William of Rubruck 1990: 210). The Mongol "magic fountain" – a favorite type of automaton ever since late antiquity – echoes earlier technologies already encountered in Constantinople and Baghdad, as well as contemporaneous developments in France (S. Farmer 2013). By now we are quite familiar with some of its elements: the tree-shape and the presence of lions spouting four rivers of enchanting beverages (rather than projecting the roar of imperial power symbolized by the Throne of Solomon).

Less studied than their Byzantine and Arabic counterparts are the Indian accounts of artificial pleasure gardens with chirping birds, buzzing bees, fountains, boats, and musicians, which abound both in fictional writings and in texts with a historiographical bent. For example, one scene from the *Śṛṅgāramañjarīkathā* ("Stories for Śṛṅgāramañjarī"), a story book attributed to the Paramāra king Bhoja of Dhārā (c. 1000–55 CE), takes place in the mechanical fountain house (*yantradhārāgṛh*). An array of artificial objects – from mechanical trees, ducks, and monkeys to black bees humming inside the bud of an open water lily – were all apparently made of precious gems and metals, and all moved and produced sounds, thus contributing to the general soundscape of the garden. Present were several female mechanical dolls (*yantraputraka*) as well, playing lutes (*vallaki*) and drums. Daud Ali has recently contextualized the text of this story book within the larger landscape of cultural contacts and diplomatic exchanges between the Abbasid and Indian worlds from the eighth century onward, noting the migration of Indian literati to the cities of the Abbasid Caliphate (Ali 2016). Such an approach has allowed him to postulate quite convincingly that, although machines had been part of Indian lore from early times (Raghavan 1952), the kinds of automata populating Bhoja's fictional and technical world (including the mechanical fountain house, the chirping birds perched on golden branches, and the female lute and drum players) correlated, at least in part, to contemporaneous preoccupations of the Byzantine, Abbasid, and Fatimid elites of the tenth and eleventh centuries.

However, neither the angel trumpeter at the top of the Mongol fountain nor the female lute-players in Bhoja's mechanical fountain house belong to the same natural world as the tree, bees, and birds, but rather represent a combination of anthropomorphic and purely organological components of the sounding automata. In particular, it is the presence of humanoids in these complex automata that is the element of utmost interest in the transcontinental fashion of constructing sound-making devices. In all these cases we are dealing with devices not designed for the general soundscapes of imperial *aulae* or as objects of diplomatic wonder – such as the trees, birds, and lions – but primarily dedicated to actual or imaginary pleasure-inducing environments and festivities. Whether solo musical instrumentalists or entire mechanical ensembles, they are conceived not just as sound-producing but actually music-making automata.

6.3 Clocks and Boats

The description of an intriguing automaton of a musical instrument appears in the ninth-century treatise *al-Āla allatī tuzammir bi-nafsihā* (*The Instrument that Plays by Itself*) by Banū (Sons of) Mūsā ibn Shākirs (H. Farmer 1931: 85–114; Samir 2015; Saliba 2015). The instrument "continuously plays whatever melody . . . we wish all by itself, sometimes in a slow rhythm . . . and sometimes in a quick rhythm, and we can also change from one melody to another whenever we so desire" (H. Farmer 1931: 88). A complex mechanical system of pipes activated by a hydraulic mechanism hidden within the body of a humanoid figure, would ensure continuous melodic production by a wind instrument (*mizmar*) or even possibly by a lute or psaltery (diagram in Chaarani 2015; reconstruction in Zielinski & Weibel 2015: 92–93). In addition, "the authors describe a method of recording the movement of the android's fingers by engraving into a large wax-coated cylinder, which then can be used to make new melody barrels" (Krzyzaniak 2016: 17). In other words, these ninth-century mechanisms appear to form the first automata capable of playing complete melodies rather than single tones, and possibly represent a forerunner of later audio recording techniques.

The fascination with hydraulic mechanisms designed to activate perpetually playing instruments continued after the decline of Abbasid patronage in the Islamicate world, as attested by Badīʿ az-Zaman Abu l-ʿIzz ibn Ismāʿīl ibn ar-Razāz al-Jazarī (1136–1206 CE/530–602 AH), polymath and chief engineer at the Artuqid palace (in present-day Diyarbakir, Turkey). In his *Kitāb fī ma'rifat al-ḥiyal al-handasiyya* ("Book of Knowledge of Ingenious Mechanical Devices"), he introduced several mechanical solutions to facilitate the correct functioning of a "perpetual flute with two spheres." Al-Jazarī's mechanism is designed to allow for two flutists, "one of whom is silent while the other blows, then the one that was blowing falls silent and the one that was silent blows" (al-Jazarī 1974: 170). In the larger context of the device as a whole, the flautists play continuously on a pool in the company of other musicians. It is a project that, according to al-Jazarī, draws upon the early twelfth-century mechanical design of al-Badīʿ al-Asṭurlābī, and the drawing of on 'old instrument', a *nāy*-like flute with eight holes and rods like moving fingers on them" (al-Jazarī 1974: 170). While we have no further information about the other musicians, all the mechanisms our author devised for this project apparently result in each flute playing only one single pitch, which is certainly much less complex a musical situation than that envisaged earlier by the Sons of Musa.

Two other devices of al-Jazarī's own invention are particularly tantalizing insofar as their musical potential is concerned. The Water-Clock of the Drummers (Figure 15), for which al-Jazarī uses a mechanism similar to the one he proposed also for the 'perpetual flute', consists of the following group of musicians (*nawba*):

> In the floor of the chamber is a platform occupying all the foreground, raised about the height of one man above the ground. On this platform are seven men: on the right two blowing trumpets, on the left two playing cymbals – the rest are drummers. The middle one has two kettle-drums (*naqqāra*) while the two to his left and right each has a drum slung over his shoulder, its head tilted upwards so that it can be struck by a drumstick (*ṣawlajān*) held in the right hand. The left hand is lowered on the other side [of the drum]. The one in the middle has a drumstick in each hand with which to strike the kettle-drums. . . . [T]he trumpeters, cymbal-players and two of the drummers are standing on their feet, not touching each other or supported by anything, while the drummer in the centre is kneeling. (al-Jazarī 1974: 42)

The name of the group of musicians, the *nawba*, could mean "a drum struck at stated hours," or "musical band playing at stated times before the palace of a king

Figure 15 Al-Jazarī (d. 1206), The Water-Clock of the Drummers. Folio from *Kitāb fī ma'rifat al-ḥiyal al-handasiyya* ("Book of Knowledge of Ingenious Mechanical Devices"); Mamluk period, 1315. Farruq ibn Abd al-Latif (calligrapher). Source: Freer Gallery of Art, Smithsonian Institution, Washington, DC: Purchase – Charles Lang Freer Endowment, F1942.10

or prince" (Hillenbrand 2011: 28). The *nawba* ceremony was already an integral part of the protocol at the caliph's court in Baghdad when a drum was struck a maximum of five times at specific intervals, as well as at lesser courts where musicians performed a certain number of times a day depending upon the prestige of the ruler. Al-Jazarī 's *nawba* performs "with a clamorous sound which is heard from afar" at every passing hour (al-Jazarī 1974: 42), which also suggests a very high status, very much in line with that of his patron, the Artuqid king of Diyar Bakr. The traditional instrumental composition of the *nawba* (winds and percussion) lends itself very well to mechanical replication, since the dominant musical components are predominantly timbral and rhythmic, and thus the automaton is anchored in the sonic and ritualistic milieu of the Islamic courts.

Sound had been a component in the telling of time long before devices such as al-Jazarī 's Water-Clock of the Drummers. Recorded among the gifts Hārūn al-Rashīd (r. 768-809) sent to Charlemagne in 807 was a "brass clock, a marvelous mechanical contraption, in which the course of the twelve hours moved according to a water clock, with as many brazen little balls, which fall down on the hour and through their fall made a cymbal ring underneath" (Scholz 1972: 87). While the Latin source provides no details as to the mechanics of the clock, al-Ghazali (d. 1111) supplies in his *Iḥyā 'Ulūm al-Dīn* ("The Revival of the Religious Sciences") much-needed information concerning the sound-production mechanics of a similar clock:

> There must be in it a device in the form of a cylinder containing a known amount of water and another hollow device placed within the cylinder [floating] above the water with a string attached. One end of the string is tied to this hollow device while its other end is tied to the bottom of a small container (*zarf*) placed above the hollow cylinder. In that container is a ball, and below it there is a shallow metal box (*ṭās*) placed in such a way that if the ball falls down from the container it falls into the metal box and its tinkling is heard.
>
> Furthermore, an aperture of a certain size is made in the bottom of the cylindrical device so that the water runs out of it little by little. As the water level is lowered, the hollow device placed on the surface of the water will be lowered, thus pulling the string attached to it and moving the container with the ball in it with a movement which nearly tilts it over. Once it is tilted, the ball rolls out of it and falls into the metal box and tinkles. At the end of each hour, a single ball falls. (Cited in Griffel 2009: 237–38)

While both the Abbasid clock and that of al-Ghazali mark the hour by sound, neither, though, matches in complexity al-Jazarī's *nawba* time-device. The only other clock that we are aware of with correspondingly complex mechanics of sound-making is the slightly earlier Chinese clock built by Su Song 蘇頌 (1020–

1101 CE) and Han Gonglian 韓公廉 in 1088 during the reign of Song emperor Zhezong 哲宗 (r. 1085–1100). Su Song listed all elements of his new clock tower in the *Xin yixiang fayao* 新儀像法要 ("New Design for an Astronomical Clock Tower") printed in 1094, with a later edition featuring meticulous illustration of the mechanics involved (tr. and comm. Needham et al. 1986). The time-telling system of Su Song's clock tower was composed of a day-and-night time-keeping wheel and a five-story pagoda. Like al-Jazarī's contraption, it included musical instruments, in this case a large bell (*zhong* 鐘), a little bell (*ling* 鈴), and a drum (*gu* 鼓), played by corresponding striking puppets with active arms. Accordingly, the "[m]ulti-cam striking mechanism worked perfectly and created correspondent musical interactions between image and sound within each story of the five-story pagoda" (Yan & Lin 2002: 24).

Al-Jazarī maintains that he invented yet another device at the bequest of his patron, "a boat which is placed on a pool during a drinking party":

> It is a handsome boat made of wood, decked over. On its stem is a platform with a dome above it, and on the platform is the seated figure of the king, with his chamberlain (*ḥājib*) standing on his right at the back of the platform. On his left is the weapon-bearer, and in front of him is a slave holding a jug and goblet, as if serving drinks. Below this is a group of boon-companions sitting to the left and to the right. In their hands and in front of them are objects [such as are used] when drinking. *On the stem of the boat is a platform, at the opposite end to the king, upon which are a flute-player, a harpist and then a tambourine-player.* Behind the platform and the slave-girls is a standing sailor, holding the boat's rudder. On either gunwale of the boat is a sailor holding an oar. This is the picture of the boat and what is upon it. (al-Jazarī 1974: 107; emphasis added) (Figure 16)

The mechanism, quite ingeniously represented in the illumination accompanying the text in most surviving manuscript copies of the treatise, consists of a system of pipes through which water was forced by a pressure pump into a camshaft where cams – whose movement was triggered by the water weight – changed the revolving movement into the two-directional displacement of a horizontal rod, which presses levers located under the instruments of automated musicians. During the continuous motion of the boat on the surface of the water, silence and sound alternate, with the musicians marking the passing of every half an hour; all this takes place in the craftily choreographed production of a spectacle that would last for several hours:

> [T]he boat is placed on the surface of a large pool, and is seldom stationary but moves in the surface of the water. All the time it moves the sailors move, because they are on axles, and the oars move it [i.e. the boat] through the water – until about half an hour has elapsed. Then, for a little while, *the flute*

Figure 16 Al-Jazarī (d. 1206), The Musical Boat. Folio from *Kitāb fī ma'rifat al-ḥiyal al-handasiyya* ("Book of Knowledge of Ingenious Mechanical Devices"); Mamluk period, 1315. Farruq ibn Abd al-Latif (calligrapher). Source: Freer Gallery of Art, Smithsonian Institution, Washington, DC: Purchase – Charles Lang Freer Endowment, F1930.73

player blows the flute and the [other] slave-girls play their instruments with sounds that are heard by the assembly. Then they fall silent. The boat moves slowly on the surface of the water until about half an hour has passed [again]. Then *the flute-player blows the flute audibly and the slave-girls play the instruments*, as happened the first time. They do not desist until they have performed about fifteen times. (al-Jazarī 1974: 107; emphasis added)

Boats loaded with musicians appear also in what remains of the *Suishi Tujing* 水飾圖經 ("Illustrations of Adornments on the Waters"), a collection of stories attributed to the late Sui period (581–618). The text describes a floating display attributed to the mechanical engineer Huang Gun 黃袞 in the service of Sui Yangdi (r. 604–18), which consisted of twelve boats arrayed with carved and inlay decorations, filled with mechanical puppets (Needham 1965: 160). Among these characters were singing girls, busily rowing oarsmen, cup-bearers and wine-pourers, dancers and tumblers, as well as musicians playing actual instruments, all moving simultaneously as if alive. The "wooden people" were performing a tune (*qu* 曲) all together by striking stone chimes (*qing* 磬) and bells (*zhong* 鍾), and by plucking zithers (*zheng* 箏 and *se* 瑟).

Huang Gun's boats are indeed eerily reminiscent of al-Jazarī's "boat of the drinking party," even though the musical instruments they respectively featured were specific to their respective regions (zithers, bells, and stone chimes vs. harp, vertical flute, and frame-drum), and even though the account of the former lacks any detail that would shed light upon the actual mechanics involved. Interestingly, however, the mechanics necessary to produce all the motions involved in these elaborate automata, in both the Chinese and the Arabic versions – rack gears, transmission chains, cam-shafts, valves of various types, etc. – display evident similarities to the Alexandrian tradition, especially to Heron's work. We cannot discard the possibility of independent development on the part of the Chinese engineers, but absent any hard evidence such a hypothesis remains untested. Nor can we ignore the possibility that, due to the chronology, conceptual and superficial (rather than mechanical) designs of certain types of automata such as these "musical boats" may just as well have traveled from China westward and reached the Arabic world by the time of al-Jazarī. Regardless, the narrative orientation and, at times, the quasi-historical and/or fictional character of the Chinese accounts – very much like those pertaining to Indian or even Byzantine cases – are evidently in stark contrast to the precise technical descriptions of the mechanics that only the Abbasid and post-Abbasid engineers produced. What is indisputable, however, is that all these tradi-tions share a fascination with creating inanimate as well as animate and humanoid replicas capable of engaging with the world of sound and musical production.

Most important for our purposes here is the fact that, just as the *nawba* in the Water-Clock of the Drummers and the striking puppets with active arms in Su Song's tower-clock, the musicians on Huang Gun's and al-Jazarī's pleasure boats are not just kinematic figurines, but musicians whose playing of instruments is intended to be heard. Not even the expert and detailed description of the mechanical aspects involved in the construction of al-Jazarī's boat provides sufficient information, however, for us to reconstruct either melodic or rhythmic aspects of these performances. All we can deduce with a high degree of certainty is that the totality of sounds, shapes, colors, and motions is absolutely indispensable for the purpose of creating the intended multisensorial experience of these mechanical marvels. Unlike the symbols of power in the Byzantine and Abbasid courtly milieu though – the chirping birds, magical trees, and roaring lions – the music-actants of our boats are pleasure-oriented mechanical replicas of categories of musicians and culturally specific instruments that were common at the courts of the Chinese and Islamicate worlds.

6.4 Players, Singers, Dancers

While the Arabic tradition is unique in its detailed technical conceptualization and mechanical realization of various sound-producing automata, the corresponding traditions of the Byzantine, Islamicate, and Mongol worlds also share direct or mediated access to Hellenistic technological thought and literature as a subject of intensive study. Their automata are also material consequences of diplomatic contact and cultural commerce among these worlds, which – at least in the case of the Byzantines and the Abbasids – led not only to active exchanges of ideas but also to technological competitions of sorts. Moreover, as we have seen, there is some evidence that the contemporaneous Indian tradition of mechanical pleasure gardens might, at least in part, be contingent upon cultural encounters with the Arabic world, and perhaps even upon older ones with the Hellenistic world (Ali 2016: 21). Any such developments happening beyond the confines of this safely circumscribed realm of Hellenistic legacy, however, are difficult to ascertain and, frankly, fraught with ideological dangers. Particularly problematic are the accounts of automata in Chinese sources. Early Ming accounts inform us, for example, that Xiao Xun 蕭洵 – the official whom the first Ming emperor ordered in 1368 to destroy the Yuan palaces and all the objects contained therein – observed that the last Yuan emperor, Toghon Temür (r. 1333–68), surrounded himself with mechanical clocks. These were in the tradition of devices such as the clocks Yi Xing 一行 (683–727) and Su Song (1020–1101) had built during the Tang and Song dynasties, respectively: self-operating tiger automata, dragon-headed devices spouting perfume mist, and several dragon-headed boats full of mechanical figures and musicians, among many others (Needham 1965: 133).

We can speculate with some confidence that at least some of these devices may have entered the Yuan court as Ilkhanid and/or Jalayirid diplomatic gifts, while others may have been locally produced according to long-established technological preoccupations. More difficult is the task of assessing the accuracy of records of alleged automata found in earlier sources, where mythology and history freely intertwined. Once again, it is regrettable that these earlier Chinese accounts of musical automata have been thus far investigated only by historians of technology who take their point of departure from the pioneering studies of Joseph Needham (1900–95), since, justifiably, they have very specific concerns. Music-oriented scholars, on the other hand, have not engaged with the subject in any meaningful way, despite the fact that many decades ago Needham also introduced us to the rich repository of literary and historiographical texts highlighting Chinese imagery and technology of mechanical music-devices. The discussion that follows highlights the benefits of interdisciplinary approaches guided by a healthy skepticism toward the long-assumed historical accuracy of these accounts. It also suggests the complex manner in which the sound-producing mechanical devices mentioned in Chinese historical texts potentially stand at the intersection of Eurasian networks of transcultural commerce and local musical practices in the first millennium of the common era.

The account of what is generally assumed to be the earliest historical mechanical musical ensemble in Chinese history, in *Xijing Zaji* 西京雜記 ("Miscellaneous Records of the Western Capital") recounts when the first Han emperor, Gaozu 高祖 (r. 202 – 195 BCE), entered the Qin palace at Xianyang 咸陽 he found:

> Twelve seated figures made of cast bronze. They were all the same height, three *chi* (ca. 3 feet), and were seated on bamboo mats, playing the *qin* (琴), *zhu* (筑), *sheng* (笙), or *yu* (竽). All [the figures] were decorated with multi-colored designs. They almost looked like real people. Underneath the bamboo mats, there were two bronze pipes, the top openings of which were several *chi* in height beyond the mats. One of the pipes was empty, and inside the other there was a rope as thick as a finger. If one blew into the empty pipe, while another person twisted the rope, all the instruments started playing, and [the effect] was no different from real music. (Olshin 2012; slightly modified)

However, *Xijing Zaji* is a collection of anecdotes from the time of the Han dynasty, compiled most likely in the early sixth century, so approximately seven centuries after the founding of the Han dynasty (Nienhauser 1978; Knechtges & Chang 2014: 1648–52). The credibility of the historical details embedded in this account has already been challenged by Zuxian Zheng, who argued a couple of decades ago that this passage cannot be read as an accurate historical record on account of both the organological details and the fictional tropes that it incorporates at different points in the narrative (Zheng 2000). A cross-disciplinary reading of this story seems to reinforce Zheng's position.

The sketchy yet suggestive details of the mechanics of sound production associated with the twelve bronze figures are nevertheless quite striking and thus, regardless of its general historical accuracy, the passage definitely carries the historical memory of what potentially was indeed an actual musical contraption. The nature of the musical instruments in the mechanical ensemble contributes to the historically ancient flavor of the passage: two zithers (the *qin* and the *zhu*) and two free-reed mouth organs (the *sheng* and the *yu*). Indeed, while both the *zhu* and the *yu* are specifically connected with ancient China (Lawergren 2000; 2017), exemplars of all four of these instruments have been unearthed together, for example in the Tomb of Marquis Yi of Zeng 曾侯乙, dated after 433 BCE (Furniss 2009: 25). The "twelve seated figures" (most likely males) were allegedly housed in the treasury of the palace – thus underscoring their being both exceptional and precious – together with other *mirabilia*: dragons with moving scales, a mirror that allowed one to see inside the body (Olshin 2012), and additional musical instruments – several other *qin* and a miraculous jade flute that when played triggered the sound of rumbling vehicles and visions of horses and mountain forests.

Surrounded by this aura of wondrousness, the twelve bronze players and their mechanical details might very well be entangled in some yet undetermined manner with the contradictory post-Han information circulating in accounts regarding the famous Twelve Golden Men (*shi'er jinren* 十二金人). According to the Chinese historian Sima Qian 司馬遷 (c. 145–86 BCE), these were the large bronze statues cast in 221 BCE from the weapons of war by the first emperor, Qin Shi Huangdi (r. 246–210 BCE), who placed them in front of his palace in the aftermath of the unification wars. Most recently, scholars have pointed out that the Twelve Golden Men embodied an entirely novel idea of sculpture, and it is possible that they were inspired by non-Chinese, Hellenistic models (Nickel 2013: 436–42; Wu 2020: 123–25). Moreover, it is only in post-Han texts that sound-making mechanical figurines start to be more frequently mentioned, at times at least in narratives contingent upon translations from Sanskrit of Buddhist texts, as our next example illustrates. In the end, our twelve players might very well prove to be not the earliest automaton in Chinese history, but a complex early sixth-century narrative in which the historical memory of Qin sculptural aesthetics triggered by encounters with Hellenism intersected with post-Han imagery pertaining to sound-producing automata of a similar source, possibly via South Asian Buddhist filiation.

Another case study comes from a collection of stories compiled by an anonymous author as late as the early fourth century and carrying the name of Liezi 列子/Lie Yukou 列圄寇 (fl. fourth century BCE), one of the three philosophers who developed the basic Daoist tenets. Although some of the material in the stories in the *Liezi* certainly comes from the formative times of Daoism, the collection itself was probably compiled around 300 CE. One of the stories tells us about a meeting between King Mu of the Zhou Dynasty (1023-957 BCE) and a mechanical engineer known as Master Yan 偃师 (Graham 1960: 110–12). The latter presents King Mu with a mechanical man he himself made: "[W]hen the craftsman pushed its cheek it sang in tune. When he clasped its hand, it danced in time; it did innumerable tricks, whatever it pleased you to ask" (Graham 1960: 110–11). Trying to prove that it was indeed an inanimate object, the craftsmen took it apart and showed the king what it was made of – leather, wood, glue, and lacquer, colored white, black, red, and blue. The king carefully inspected all the organs convincing himself that it was all artificial and no motion or sound would occur while the mechanical man was in pieces. Once it was put back together, it regained the capacity for singing and dancing rhythmically. No activation mechanism is even mentioned, let alone described.

Although positioned in the context of a Daoist work, the narrative is very similar to a *jataka* story in *Sheng jing* 生經 ("The Sutra of Jatakas") rendered into Chinese by Dharmarakṣa in the year 258 CE (Ji 1950; cited in Zürcher 2007: 275). There are other Buddhist narratives that circulated in South Asia and referenced what appear to be mechanical humanoids, but, while all these humanoids seem to embody echoes of Hellenistic technology, none of them is a music-making contraption (Beguš 2020). By itself, this makes our story quite exceptional. The Buddhist rendition of the story makes clear that the main protagonist (this time the middle son of a king) comes across the "wooden man" during his travel to a foreign land, in the context of his encounter with a king who appreciated skillful artifices (Chavannes 1911 [3]: 170–72).

The notion of a "foreign land" endures in the *Liezi* story. Here, King Mu of Zhou undertakes a journey to the West, passing Kunlun 崑崙 mountain but not reaching Mount Yan 弇山 (the mythological place of the setting sun). On his way back, but before he reaches the Middle Kingdom (China), he comes upon the craftsman Master Yan. In sum, in both versions the automaton belongs to a culture perceived as foreign, which in the case of the Chinese version is clearly placed to the West of the Middle Kingdom. Moreover, King Mu's encounter with the automaton occurs as part of his mythological tour of the Western lands and his meeting with Xiwangmu 西王母 (the "Queen Mother of the West") whose abode was Mount Kunlun. The most extended narration of this journey appears in the *Mu Tianzi Zhuan* 穆天子傳 ("Tale of Mu, Son of Heaven"), a text dating back to a period between the fifth and the fourth century BCE but which does not contain our story (Rippa 2014: 151). While the tale of the automaton itself seems to belong to an Indian Buddhist stratum accessed in China around the middle of the third century, the story itself in *Liezi* is cast as an offshoot of the mythological tradition surrounding King Mu's journey, a "fine example of the Chinese practice of euhemerization (turning mythical people and events into apparently historical ones)" (Cahill 1993: 14).

Underscoring the Western foreignness of the automaton as it is linked with the lands of Queen Mother of the West – and let us not forget that we are dealing with an automaton that sang and danced, hence had musical capabilities – are some intriguing music-iconographical details associated with the goddess during the Han era. Several instances of her depiction in Han art feature the *aulos*, the iconic Greek and Hellenistic double pipe. All these depictions appear on objects produced in the aftermath of Zhang Qian's 張騫 expedition to Central Asia (138–126 BCE) and are exclusively linked to the Queen Mother of the West's iconography (Furniss & Hagel 2017). One might infer, therefore, that

Chinese direct or indirect experience with the Greek *aulos* was possibly mediated by the Hellenistic traces in contemporaneous cultures of Inner Asia (such as that of Bactria and the Kushan empire) and further that, likewise, the *jataka*-derived tale of a musical humanoid automaton projected upon King Mu's mythological journey to the west was the product of similar encounters.

Rather than assigning them to technologies of the Qin and Zhou eras, the more plausible interpretation for the twelve instrumentalists and the singing/dancing man of the Western lands is that they are mytho-historical objects, which – as a consequence of direct and indirect encounters with Central Asian Hellenism and translations of Buddhist texts – partake in the post-Han mediated awareness of technological imagery from the "western lands."

6.5 Ὄργανον, *Organum*, and the 'Booming Sheng'

In the context of cultural encounters, interpreting the presence of musical instruments and their visual representations can effectively draw on the sociological concept of "boundary objects," introduced by Susan Leigh Star and James Griesemer several decades ago; music objects as well as their visual representations stand as "objects which are both plastic enough to adapt to local needs and constraints of the several parties employing them, yet robust enough to maintain a common identity across sites" (Star & Griesemer 1989: 393). In the conceptual framework of cultural encounter and exchange, the adoption (or at times, rejection), transformation, and/or integration of musical instruments, together with their visual representations, stand witness to processes of cultural translation marked by intercultural dynamics as varied as they are complex. In its long history articulated by nodes of imperial diplomatic instances of gift exchanges, the organ is such a boundary object. Moreover, as the most complex of all premodern mechanical instruments, the organ occupied a position of prestige from the early times of the Byzantine empire. Although it functioned on mechanical principles shared with the kind of automata discussed earlier, the organ inhabited a conceptually different sonic world. It represented a world of sound organized according to musical principles and the level of control the human player has upon the multitude of possible choices.

Just like the automata linked to the imperial throne, pneumatic organs – instruments provided with bellows that push pressurized air through pipes to produce sound – were part and parcel of the Byzantine display of power. Byzantine sources of the tenth century mention two golden organs which accompanied the ceremonies performed by the emperor at the reception of foreign ambassadors. Moreover, silver organs associated with the Blues and the Greens – by the fifth century the two state-sponsored and administered corporations responsible for the organization of every sort of public entertainment – are also mentioned in the context of festive occasions, as are organs participant in the rituals for the day before the opening of the chariot races in the Hippodrome. In fact, one of the earliest representations of pneumatic organs in Byzantine art is carved on the fourth-century base of the obelisk found at the Hippodrome itself. At the very bottom of the carving, a row of musicians and female dancers is flanked by two organs, each provided with two operators of the bellows as well as an organ player (Figure 17).

Numerous historical accounts attest to the instrument's expansive musical capabilities. Harun ben-Jahja, for example – an Arab prisoner of war who witnessed the feast Basil I (r. 867–86) gave for Muslim captives – offered the following account:

> Then they bring a thing which is called *al-urgana* . . . . This is an object made out of a square of wood after the manner of an oil-press, covered with strong leather, into which sixty pipes of copper are put. The part of the pipes outside the leather is covered with gold, so that only a little of them can be seen, because each pipe is only a little longer than the one before. At one side of the square object is a hole; into this a pair of bellows is put, like the bellows of a forge. . . . Two men now start to blow the organ, and the master comes and plays the pipes; and each pipe sings according to its length, sounding in honor of the Emperor, while all the people sit at their tables. (Wellesz 1961: 106)

Additional evidence from Arab sources suggests that Byzantine organs were capable of sophisticated and varied sound projections. At the beginning of the tenth century, for example, Ibn Rusta reports that the organist plays upon the sixty brass pipes of the organ "and each pipe he makes to speak in turn, according to what he plays" (H. Farmer 1931: 59).

To the Byzantines, the organ was both an imperial symbol that rendered them as the true heir of ancient Rome, and an exotic gift to be made in order to impress foreign rulers. As a diplomatic gift, the organ "represented technology not available to its recipients, and thus had the potential to demonstrate the superiority of the sender" (Brubaker 2004: 175). This is most likely the spirit in which the East Roman Emperor Constantine V (r. 741–75) sent an embassy to the Frankish king Pepin (r. 751–68) with impressive gifts that included an organ, heralded in Frankish chronicles as something not previously seen in the kingdom. According to a single later and somewhat doubtful report with hyperbolic language, Charlemagne received another organ in 812, an instrument with bronze pipes, bellows of bull leather and three sound effects. While Latin sources are at times contradictory as to both the provenance and the morphology of the instrument, including the means through which such instruments may have made their way from Byzantium to Carolingian lands, the transcultural

Figure 17 Dancers and instrumentalists flanked by two organs (bottom register). 'Obelisk of Theodosius I', Hippodrome, Istanbul, Turkey (fourth century CE). Source: Gabriela Currie.

journey of a musical instrument of Byzantine origin to the Western courts is a transformative moment in the history of both Carolingian musical traditions and that of the instrument itself. Most importantly, in Byzantium the organ was part of the imperial paraphernalia and used primarily for secular ceremonies, not in church. In the Latin world, the monastic revival in the late tenth century was in all likelihood a factor in the transformation of the organ into an ingenious object for the use of the clergy, with an increasingly strong music-theoretical foundation. Ultimately, its tunings, morphology, social function, and performative practices were all renegotiated in the Carolingian and post-Carolingian cultural environment, and through cultural acceptance, transformation, and integration, the organ of the Byzantines became that of the Latins and thus it acquired a life of its own in the Western European musical practices and imagination.

With reference to music organology, the Arabic term *arghanūn* can be used both as conceptual placeholder as well as a name for a specific instrument. Persian-language poetry teems with references to *arghanūn*; Ḥāfeẓ (d. 1390), for example, mentions it often in his *ghazals* and many times in association with the harmonies of music and the celestial spheres. Elsewhere without doubt – as attested by numerous references and descriptions in Arabic and Persian-language writings – the specific musical instrument that the term *arghanūn* (and etymologically related variants) most often denoted was the Byzantine/Latin organ. For instance, the Timurid music theorist al-Marāghī uses the term *arghanūn* in reference to an instrument often used by Europeans (*ahl-e farang*) and provides a detailed description of the organ in his *Jāme'-al-alḥān*. Nonetheless, not everyone among the writers in the Islamicate world who mentioned the *arghanūn* (organ) had direct (visual and aural) experience with the instrument; al-Tawḥīdī (d. 1023), for example, one of the main witnesses of the intellectual activity of eleventh-century Baghdad, stated that: "for the Byzantine organ (*al-urghan al-rūmī*), we must confess that we have not heard it and know it only from texts and paintings (*muṣawwaran*); al-Kindī and others wrote about the instrument, but not about how to play it" (Puerta Vílchez 2017: 217). Although it made an impression on the various Arabic, Persian, and later Mongol rulers, travelers, philosophers, and poets, the Byzantine organ remained in the Islamicate world an instrument of music theory or an exotic object of foreign practices.

An altogether different set of imperial cultural dynamics surround the introduction to China of an organ during the Zhongtong 中統 era (1260–64) of the reign of Kublai Khan (r. 1260–94). According to some Chinese sources, the organ arrived "from the lands of the West" (*xiyu* 西域) or "Islamic lands" (*huihui guo* 回回國), thus very likely from the lands under the rule of Kublai's younger brother Hülegü, the first Ilkhan (r. 1260–65), who had conquered Baghdad in 1258 and subsequently attempted repeatedly to establish a Franco-Mongol alliance against the Mamluks. The timing itself is interesting for, in the context of the Byzantine world, it appears that the organ had fallen victim to the devastation brought upon Constantinople by the Latin crusaders in 1204 and had not been reintroduced at celebrations carried out in Constantinople after the city had been restored to Byzantine rule in 1224.

Chinese sources refer to this instrument as the "Booming Sheng" (*Xinglong sheng* 興隆笙) using as organological referent the familiar Chinese mouth organ, the *sheng* (a mouth-blown free-reed instrument). Three fourteenth-century accounts provide a description of the instrument and the manner of producing sound, with complementary details and little contradictory information. According to these sources, the Booming Sheng was made of *nan* wood (楠木), shaped like a double screen inlaid with golden ornaments, and inside with a hollow chest like the air chamber of the *sheng*; it was equipped with ninety pipes of purple bamboo arranged in fifteen ranks each with six pipes arranged across, and from the foot of the chest to the top of the pipes it was about five feet high; the pipes were filled at the ends with brass apricot leaves, and it stood on a pedestal surrounded with lions and elephants (according to one of the sources); a person activated the two extant bellows while another one played the pipes (summarized from Moule & Galpin 1926: 194).

The pitches generated by this instrument – which was possibly manufactured in Syria or Baghdad and, if so, it would thus most likely have followed Arabic tuning, possibly involving microtones – did not align well with the standard Chinese tuning system. Zeng Xiu 鄭秀, an official at the Music Bureau (*Yuchen yueyuan* 玉宸樂院) retuned them therefore according to the local usage; the new instrument was also provided with mechanical peacocks activated by a player inside the body of the instrument (Gimm 2012: 450). The morphological alteration of the instrument for the purpose of bringing it closer in line with local aesthetics and musical standards may indeed be seen as a set of adaptive processes not unlike those undertaken by the Carolingians and their successors. The Booming Sheng quickly found a place in the grand orchestra at the Yuan palace, among other instruments such as lutes (*pipa* and *huobusi*), zithers (*zheng* and *qin*), fiddles (*huqin*), drums (*zhanggu, hegu,* et al.*),* flutes (*xiao longdi,* et al.), and other instruments (Lam 1994: 179, n. 33). As part of the banquet music (*yanyue*) at the Yuan court, the organ seems to have been the instrument of reference since when the organ sounded, all the instruments began playing and they fell silent as soon as the organ fell silent.

Although several copies seem to have been manufactured at the Yuan court on the basis of the Western model, and in spite of the success the instrument experienced at the Yuan court proper, the Booming Sheng vanishes from the records after the fourteenth century, and not until the Jesuit missions of the seventeenth century did China encounter European musical instruments again. In fact, the great organ of the Western lands functioned more like a curiosity item, integrated in the orchestra more as a symbol of the Yuan entanglements with the larger Mongol world west of China, an item that failed to take root in the musical culture of China in the post-Yuan world. Ultimately, unlike the Byzantine-Carolingian organ that found a new home in the Latin West, the Yuan organ was a short-lived boundary object that, despite its aesthetic appeal and mechanical appreciation as well as its imperial support, quickly fell into desuetude and disappeared from the Chinese historical record.

7 Epilogue

The five different stories selected for this Element have introduced the reader to the intriguingly complex premodern history of musical encounters and exchanges across Eurasia. Each case has highlighted specific dynamics in the circulation of musical instruments and practices, following multidirectional trajectories through both settled imperial geographies and expansive nomadic cultures, all viewed through the lens of extant textual, visual, and archaeological sources.

Musical cosmopolitanism, cultural identity, and transcontinental circulation have emerged as themes throughout our five stories, which highlight the insights that selected musical objects, concepts, or exchanges can provide into the particular historical manifestations of these phenomena. The kind of musical cosmopolitanism witnessed in the Sui and Tang capital of Chang'an, for example, was by and large qualitatively distinct from that which flourished in the contemporaneous kingdom of Kucha. On the one hand, imperial Chinese cultural geographies – constructions of both the historical present and the mythological past – served as the operating principle in the organization and codification of the courtly performing divisions together with their constitutive instruments, costumes, and music and dance repertoires from diverse areas of Eurasia, and encompassed the courtly enthusiastic embrace of the Sogdian female whirling dance. At the same time, the Sogdian male leaping dance flourished in the context of private gatherings of Tang literati, and was incorporated in the iconography of funerary objects linked with members of the Sogdian communities in China as cultural identity markers. Kuchean cosmopolitanism, on the other hand, emerged at the dynamic intersection of Indian and Irano-Sogdian musical domains – material and conceptual – as well as Buddhist and Zoroastrian belief systems as performative contexts. None of the elements of Kuchean musical practices as documented in local textual and visual sources was noticeably regulated by the social elites of the kingdom, but rather arose in resonance with the diverse ethnic, religious, and linguistic composition of its population.

Other facets of musical identity permeate the story of the *qopuz,* a key organological marker of Turkic peoples throughout their migrations, and a prime example of the ambiguous relationship that can exist between instrumental nomenclature and morphology. Unlike the stories centered on Chang'an and Kucha, this story takes us on the road beyond any particular urban node in the Eurasian network, thus favoring a transcontinental perspective contingent upon the histories of various Turkic peoples as they moved across Eurasia for centuries – from the Altai to the Tian Shan and Crimea, and from the Uighur Qocho to the Timurid Herat – in a grand ethnolinguistic saga. Premised upon even broader currents of transcontinental circulation, our last story relates the Eurasian peripatetics of real or imagined objects that embodied the longstanding human fascination with creating complex lifelike mechanical sound-producing devices. Across Eurasia for many centuries, trees teeming with singing birds, musical fountains, roaring lions, and musical clocks filled the air of imperial courts with mechanical sounds of power and wonder, while human replicas designed to captivate audiences with their dancing and instrumental abilities populated technological and mythological imaginaries. In this context, the imperial journeys of the organ – a music-mechanical marvel requiring human agency to organize and control sound according to culturally specific musical principles – serves to map the broader enduring circulation patterns of diplomatic gift exchange all the way from Byzantium to Yuan China.

An Element such as this can only sample the musical riches of the Eurasian world writ large, sketching the general outlines of specific transmission networks for a handful of musical instruments and practices, in an effort to bring a global perspective to bear upon the varied, and unevenly distributed, sources at our disposal. Our choice of stories has focused on overland exchanges of goods and ideas, yet it is well worth noting that a considerable portion of the overall long-distance Eurasian trade was carried out by sea, albeit connecting largely different groups of people and thus requiring different historical approaches (see for example Arsenio Nicolas's analysis of maritime archaeology of insular Southeast Asian trade [Nicolas 2011; 2012]). The insights gained over the course of our overland journeys thus suggest the promise of investigating parallel sea routes, whose different geographies would necessarily bring Africa into the discussion of musical encounters and exchanges, with Malay as well as Arab trading networks. For the time being, our Silk Road stories of overland transcultural musical commerce – firmly grounded in the shifting sands, windy steppes, and rocky slopes of Central Asia – represent a first step in the broader interdisciplinary exploration of musical encounter and exchange from a truly global perspective.

References

Ali, Daud. 2016. "Bhoja's Mechanical Garden: Translating Wonder across the Indian Ocean Circa 800–1100 CE." *History of Religions* 55(4), 460–93.

al-Jazarī. 1974. *The Book of Knowledge of Ingenious Mechanical Devices [by] Ibn al-Razzaz al Jazari.* Translated by Donald R. Hill. Dordrecht/Boston: Reidel.

al-Kāšġarī, Maḥmūd. 1982. *Compendium of the Turkic Dialects: (Dīwān Luġāt at-Turk).* Edited by Robert Dankoff and James Kelly. Cambridge, MA: Harvard University Print Office.

Ambrosetti, Nadia. 2019. "Cultural Roots of Technology: An Interdisciplinary Study of Automated Systems from the Antiquity to the Renaissance." PhD thesis, University of Milan.

Barthold, Vasilii V., and J. M. Rogers. 1970. "The Burial Rites of the Turks and the Mongols." *Central Asiatic Journal* 14(1), 195–227.

Becker, Judith. 1988. "Earth, Fire, Śakti and the Javanese Gamelan." *Ethnomusicology* 32(3), 385–91.

Beguš, Nina. 2020. "A Tocharian Tale from the Silk Road: A Philological Account of the Painter and the Mechanical Maiden and Its Resonances with the Western Canon." *Journal of the Royal Asiatic Society* 30(4), 681–706.

Bodrogligeti, András J. E. 1987. "A Masterpiece of Central Asian Turkic Satire: Aḥmadi's *A Contest of String Instruments.*" *Ural-Altaische Jahrbücher* 59, 55–88.

Borroni, Massimiliano. 2019. "Samāġa Performances in Third/Ninth-Century Abbasid Courts." *Bulletin of SOAS* 82(2), 289–302.

Brett, Gerard. 1954. "The Automata in the Byzantine 'Throne of Solomon.'" *Speculum* 29(3), 477–87.

Brubaker, Leslie. 2004. "The Elephant and the Ark: Cultural and Material Interchange across the Mediterranean in the Eighth and Ninth Centuries." *Dumbarton Oaks Papers* 58, 175–95.

Cahill, Suzanne. 1993. *Transcendence and Divine Passion: The Queen Mother of the West in Medieval China.* Stanford: Stanford University Press.

Cao Yin, ed. 2013. *A Silk Road Saga: The Sarcophagus of Yu Hong.* Sydney: Art Gallery of New South Wales in association with the Shanxi Museum.

Chaarani, Mona Sanjakdar. 2015. "The Automatic Mechanical Hydraulic Organ of the Banū Mūsā ibn Shākir." In *Allah's Automata: Artifacts of the Arab-Islamic Renaissance (800–1200),* edited by Siegfried Zielinski and Peter Weibel, 86–91. Ostfildern: Hatje Cantz Verlag.

Chavannes, Édouard, ed. and tr. 1911. *Cinq cents contes et apologues: extraits du Tripiṭaka chinois et traduits en français par Édouard Chavannes.* 3 vols. Paris: E. Leroux.

Chavannes, Édouard. 1914. "Une version chinoise du conte bouddhique de Kalyânamkara et Pâpamkara." *T'oung Pao* 15(4), 469–500.

Chen, Sanping. 2012. *Multicultural China in the Early Middle Ages.* Philadelphia: University of Pennsylvania Press.

Cheng, Bonnie. 2010. "The Space Between: Locating 'Culture.'" *Ars Orientalis* 38, 81–120.

Chou Wen-Chung. 1976. "Chinese Historiography and Music: Some Observations." *The Musical Quarterly* 62(2), 218–40.

Chwolson, Daniel. 1886. Syrische Grabinschriften aus Semirjetschie. *Mémoires de l'academie Imperiale des Sciences de St.-Petersbourg.* Série VII, tome 34(4). St. Petersburg: Académie Impériale des Sciences.

Chwolson, Daniel. 1897. *Syrisch-Nestorianische Grabinschriften Aus Semirjetschie: Neue Folge.* St. Petersburg: Académie Impériale des Sciences.

Clauson, Gerard. 1972. *An Etymological Dictionary of Pre-Thirteenth-Century Turkish.* Oxford: Clarendon Press.

Compareti, Matteo, and Simone Cristoforetti. 2007. *New Elements on the Chinese Scene in the "Hall of the Ambassadors" at Afrāsyāb and a Reconsideration of "Zoroastrian" Calendar.* Eurasiatica no. 78. Venice: Dept. of Eurasian Studies publications, Ca' Foscari University.

Cook, Scott. 1995. "Yue Ji – Record of Music: Introduction, Translation, Notes, and Commentary." *Asian Music* 26(2), 1–96.

Courant, Maurice. 1913. "Chine et Corée: Essai historique sur la musique classique de la chinois avec un appendice relatif a la musique coréenne." In *Encyclopédie de la Musique et Dictionnaire du Conservatoire, Première Partie: Histoire de la Musique Antiquité – Moyen Age,* edited by Albert Lavignac, 77–251. Paris: Libraire Delagrave.

Currie, Gabriela. 2020. "Sounds from under the Shifting Sands: Reflections on Kuchean Music Culture of the Sixth and Seventh Centuries." In *Crossing Borders: Musical Change and Exchange through Time. Publications of the ICTM Study Group for Music Archaeology,* vol. 2, edited by Arnd Adje Both, Jon Hughes, and Matthias Stöckli, 223–42. Berlin: Ekho Verlag.

Currie, Gabriela. (In press). "Language, Image, and the Early Musical World of Kucha." In *Il patrimonio musicale nella storia della cultura dall'Antichità alla prima età moderna/Music as Cultural Heritage from Antiquity to Early Modern Age,* edited by Nicoletta Guidobaldi and Donatella Restani. Bologna: Bononia University Press.

Curta, Florin. 2019. *Eastern Europe in the Middle Ages (500–1300).* Leiden: Brill.

Delacour, Catherine, and Pénélope Riboud. 2004. "Un monument funéraire en pierre (Chine, VIe s.) au Musée Guimet." *Arts Asiatiques* 59, 161–65.

Deluz, Vincent. 2017. "De la clepsydre animée à l'horloge mécanique à automates, entre Antiquité et Moyen Âge." In *Autour des machines de Vitruve. L'ingénerie romaine: textes, archéologie et restitution*, edited by Sophie Madeleine and Philippe Fleury, 173–94. Caen: Presses universitaires de Caen.

Dessì, Paola. 2010. "Organi, orologi e automi musicali: oggetti sonori per il potere." *Acta Musicologica* 82(1), 21–47.

DeWoskin, Kenneth J. 1982. *A Song for One or Two: Music and the Concept of Art in Early China*. Ann Arbor, MI: Center for Chinese Studies, University of Michigan.

Dickens, Mark. 2016. "More Gravestones in Syriac Script from Tashkent, Panjikent and Ashgabat." In *Winds of Jingjiao: Studies on Syriac Christianity in China and Central Asia*, edited by Li Tang and Dietmar W. Winkler, 105–30. Vienna: LIT Verlag.

Doerfer, Gerhard. 1967. *Türkische und mongolische Elemente im Neupersischen: unter besonderer Berücksichtigung älterer neupersischer Geschichtsquellen, vor allem der Mongolen- und Timuridenzeit: Türkische Elemente: ǧī bis kāf*. Wiesbaden: Franz Steiner Verlag.

Eckardt, Hans. 1953. "Somakusa." *Sinologica: Review of Chinese Culture and Science* 3, 174–89.

Esin, Emel. 1970. "'Ay-Bitiği': The Court Attendants in Turkish Iconography." *Central Asiatic Journal* 14(1/3), 78–117.

Farmer, Henry. 1931. *The Organ of the Ancients: From Eastern Sources (Hebrew, Syriac and Arabic)*. London: Reeves.

Farmer, Sharon. 2013. "Aristocratic Power and the 'Natural' Landscape: The Garden Park at Hesdin, ca. 1291–1302." *Speculum* 88(3), 644–80.

Featherstone, Michael. 2007. "Δι' Ἔνδειξιν: Display in Court Ceremonial (De Cerimoniis II,15)." In *The Material and the Ideal: Essays in Mediaeval Art and Archaeology in Honour of Jean-Michel Spieser*, edited by Anthony Cutler and Arietta Papaconstantinou, 75–112. Leiden: Brill.

Furniss, Ingrid. 2009. "Unearthing China's Informal Musicians: An Archeological and Textual Study of the Shang to Tang Periods." *Yearbook for Traditional Music* 41, 23–41.

Furniss, Ingrid, and Stefan Hagel. 2017. "Xiwangmu's Double Pipe: A Musical Link to the Far Hellenist West?" *Imago Musicae* 29, 7–32.

Garfias, Robert. 1975. *Music of a Thousand Autumns: The Tōgaku Style of Japanese Court Music*. Berkeley: University of California Press.

Gaulier, Simone. 1973. "Aspects iconographiques des croyances eschatologiques dans le Bassin du Tarim d'après deux documents Pelliot." *Arts Asiatiques* 28(1), 165–84.

Gershkovich, Yakov. 2011. "Korkut's Heritage in the Cuman Milieu of the North Pontic Region." *Ukrainian Archaeology*, 81–90.

Gimm, Martin. 1966. *Das Yueh-Fu Tsa-Lu des Tuan An-Chieh: Studien zur Geschichte von Musik, Schauspiel und Tanz in der T'ang-Dynastie.* Wiesbaden: Otto Harrassowitz.

Gimm, Martin. 2012. "Eine Westliche Pfeifenorgel im China der Mongolenzeit." *Zeitschrift Der Deutschen Morgenländischen Gesellschaft* 162(2), 439–56.

Golden, Peter, ed. 2000. *The King's Dictionary: The Rasûlid Hexaglot – Fourteenth Century Vocabularies in Arabic, Persian, Turkic, Greek, Armenian, and Mongol.* Leiden: Brill.

Graham, Angus Charles, tr. 1960. *The Book of Lieh-Tzŭ.* London: Murray.

Grenet, Frantz, Pénélope Riboud, and Yang Junkai. 2004. "Zoroastrian Scenes on a Newly Discovered Sogdian Tomb in Xi'an, Northern China." *Studia Iranica* 33, 273–84.

Griffel, Frank. 2009. *Al-Ghazali's Philosophical Theology.* Oxford: Oxford University Press.

Grünwedel, Albert. 1912. *Altbuddhistische Kultstätten in Chinesisch-Turkistan Bericht über archäologische Arbeiten von 1906 bis 1907 bei Kucha, Qarašahr und in der Oase Turfan.* Berlin: G. Reimer.

Hamilton, James Russell. 1971. *Le conte bouddhique du bon et du mauvais prince en version ouïgoure: manuscrits ouïgours de Touen-Houang.* Paris: Klincksieck.

Hansen, Valerie. 2015. *Silk Road: A New History.* Oxford and New York: Oxford University Press.

Hillenbrand, Carole. 2011. "Aspects of the Court of the Great Seljuqs." In *The Seljuqs: Politics, Society and Culture*, edited by Christian Lange and Songül Mecit, 22–38. Edinburgh: Edinburgh University Press.

Hu, Jun. 2017. "Global Medieval at the 'End of the Silk Road,' circa 756 CE: The Shōsō-in Collection in Japan." *The Medieval Globe* 3(2), 177–202.

Ibn Battuta. 1994. *The Travels of Ibn Battuta: A. D. 1325–1354*, vol. 4, tr. by Hamilton A. R. Gibb and Charles F. Beckingham. London: The Hakluyt Society.

Ji Xianlin. 1950. "Liezi and Buddhist Sutras – A Note on the Author of Liezi and the Date of Its Composition." *Studia Serica* 9(1), 18–32.

Juliano, Annette L., and Judith A. Lerner. 1997. "Cultural Crossroads: Central Asian and Chinese Entertainers on the Miho Funerary Couch." *Orientations* 28(9), 72–78.

Juliano, Annette L., and Judith A Lerner. 2001. *Monks and Merchants: Silk Road Treasures from Northwest China*. New York and London: Harry N. Abrams.

Kapstein, Matthew T. 2009. *Buddhism Between Tibet and China*. Somerville, MA: Wisdom Publications.

Kishibe Shigeo. 1940. "The Origin of the P'i P'a: With Particular Reference to the Five-Stringed P'i P'a Preserved in the Shôsôin." *Transactions of the Asiatic Society of Japan* 19, 259–304.

Kishibe Shigeo. 1960. *A Historical Study of the Music of the T'ang Dynasty*. Tokyo: Tokyo University Press.

Knechtges, David R., and Taiping Chang, eds. 2014. *Ancient and Early Medieval Chinese Literature. Part III. Ancient and Early Medieval Chinese Literature*, vols. 3–4. Leiden: Brill.

Krzyzaniak, Michael. 2016. "Timbral Learning for Musical Robots." PhD thesis, Arizona State University, Tempe.

Kuun, Géza. 1981. *Codex Cumanicus*. Repr. Budapest: MTAK (Hungarian Academy of Sciences Library).

La Vaissière, Étienne de. 2005. *Sogdian Traders: A History*. Leiden: Brill.

Lam, Joseph S. C. 1994. "'There is no Music in Chinese Music History': Five Court Tunes from the Yuan Dynasty (AD 1271–1368)." *Journal of the Royal Musical Association* 119(2), 165–88.

Lawergren, Bo. 2000. "Strings." In *Music in the Age of Confucius*, edited by Jenny F. So, 65–86. Washington, DC: Smithsonian Institution.

Lawergren, Bo. 2010. "Ancient Harps near Dunhuang." In *Conservation of Ancient Sites on the Silk Road: Second International Conference on the Conservation of Grotto Sites, Mogao Grottoes, Dunhuang, People's Republic of China, June 28–July 3, 2004*, edited by Agnew Neville, 117–24. Los Angeles: Getty Conservation Center.

Lawergren, Bo. 2017. "Foreign Instruments in Early China." Lecture, Shanghai Conservatory of Music, September 15, 2017, www.academia.edu/38329633/Foreign_Instruments_in_Early_China_pdf.

Lawergren, Bo, Eckhard Neubauer, and M. H. Kadyrov. 2000. "Music and Musicology, Theatre and Dance." In *History of Civilizations of Central Asia: The Age of Achievement: A.D. 750 to the End of the Fifteenth Century; The Achievements*, edited by Clifford. E. Bosworth and Muhammad S. Asimov, IV/2: 590–606. Paris: UNESCO Publishing.

Lerner, Judith. 2005. *Aspects of Assimilation: The Funerary Practices and Furnishings of Central Asians in China*. Sino-Platonic Papers 168. Philadelphia: University of Pennsylvania Department of East Asian Languages and Civilizations.

Lerner, Judith. 2011. "Zoroastrian Funerary Beliefs and Practices Known from the Sino-Sogdian Tombs in China." *The Silk Road* 9, 18–25.

Li Mei. 2014. "Adaptations of Harps Reflected in Murals of the Chinese Western Regions." *Music in Art* 39(1–2), 43–55.

Liang Mingyue. 1984. "Review of Laurence Picken et al., eds., *Music from the Tang Court.*" *Ethnomusicology* 28(2), 359–62.

Liang Mingyue. 1985. *Music of the Billion: An Introduction to Chinese Musical Culture.* Wilhelmshaven: Heinrichshofen Edition.

Linder, Gunnar Jinmei. 2012. *Deconstructing Tradition in Japanese Music: A Study of Shakuhachi, Historical Authenticity and Transmission of Tradition.* PhD thesis, Stockholm University.

Liu, Mau-Tsai. 1958. *Die chinesischen Nachrichten zur Geschichte der Ost-Türken (T'u-küe).* Wiesbaden: Harrassowitz.

Liu, Mau-Tsai. 1969. *Kutscha und seine Beziehungen zu China vom 2. Jh. v. bis zum 6. Jh. n. Chr.* Wiesbaden: O. Harrassowitz.

Lo Muzio, Ciro. (In press). "Iranian Dancers in Sino-Sogdian Funerary Reliefs. Some Notes on the Hutengwu." In *Proceedings of the International Academic Conference on Sogdians on the Silk Road, Xi'an, June 25–27, 2021.*

Lo Muzio, Ciro. 2019. "Persian 'Snap': Iranian Dancers in Gandhāra." In *The Music Road: Coherence and Diversity in Music from the Mediterranean to India,* edited by Reinhard Strohm. Proceedings of the British Academy 223, 71–86. Oxford: Oxford University Press.

MacKenzie, David N. n.d. "Codex Cumanicus." In *Encyclopedia Iranica,* 885–86. www.iranicaonline.org/articles/codex-cumanicus. Accessed December 16, 2020.

Mahler, Eduard. 1887. "Über eine in einer syrischen Grabinschrift erwähnte Sonnenfinsterniss." *Sitzungsberichte Der Kaiserlichen Akademie Der Wissenschaften* 95, 359–66.

Mair, Victor H. 1994. *The Columbia Anthology of Traditional Chinese Literature.* New York: Columbia University Press.

Mango, Cyril. 1997. *The Art of the Byzantine Empire 312–1453: Sources and Documents.* London: University of Toronto Press; Medieval Academy of America.

Mayor, Adrienne. 2018. *Gods and Robots: Myths, Machines, and Ancient Dreams of Technology.* Princeton, NJ: Princeton University Press.

Mertens, Matthias. 2019. "Did Richthofen Really Coin 'the Silk Road'?" *The Silk Road* 17, 1–9.

Miho Museum. 1997. *Miho Museum.* [S.I.]: Miho Museum.

Millward, James A. 2007. *Eurasian Crossroads: A History of Xinjiang.* New York: Columbia University Press.

Moule, Arthur C. and Francis W. Galpin. 1926. "A Western Organ in Medieval China." *The Journal of the Royal Asiatic Society of Great Britain and Ireland* 2, 193–211.

Myers, John. 1992. *The Way of the Pipa: Structure and Imagery in Chinese Lute Music*. Kent, OH: Kent State University Press.

Needham, Joseph. 1965. *Science and Civilisation in China*, vol. 4, *Physics and Physical Technology*, part 2, *Mechanical Engineering*. Cambridge: Cambridge University Press.

Needham, Joseph, Wang Ling, and Derek De Solla Price. 1986. *Heavenly Clockwork: The Great Astronomical Clocks of Medieval China*. 2nd ed. Cambridge: Cambridge University Press.

von Neustadt, Heinrich. 1906. *Heinrichs von Neustadt "Apollonius von Tyrland" Nach der Gothaer Handschrift, "Gottes Zukunft" und "Visio Philiberti" Nach Der Heidelberger Handschrift, Herausgegeben von S. Singer*, edited by Samuel Singer. Berlin: Weidmann.

Nickel, Lukas. 2013. "The First Emperor and Sculpture in China." *Bulletin of the School of Oriental and African Studies* 76(3), 413–47.

Nicolas, Arsenio. 2011. "Musical Exchange between India and Southeast Asia." In *Early Interactions between South and Southeast Asia: Reflections on Cross-Cultural Exchange*, edited by Pierre-Yves Manguin, A. Mani, and Geoff Wade, 343–65. Institute of Southeast Asian Studies.

Nicolas, Arsenio. 2012. "Lineages, Networks, Centers and Peripheries: Musical Exchange in Maritime Asia." In *Understanding Confluences and Contestations, Continuities and Changes: Towards Transforming Society and Empowering People: The Work of 2009–2010 API Fellows*, 226–38. The Nippon Foundation.

Nienhauser, William H. 1978. "Once Again, the Authorship of the *Hsi-Ching Tsa-Chi* (Miscellanies of the Western Capital)." *Journal of the American Oriental Society* 98(3), 219–36.

Ning Qiang. 2004. *Art, Religion, and Politics in Medieval China: The Dunhuang Cave of the Zhai Family*. Honolulu: University of Hawai'i Press.

Olshin, Benjamin B. 2012. "A Revealing Reflection: The Case of the Chinese Emperor's Mirror." *Icon* 18, 122–41.

Ortolani, Benito. 1995. *The Japanese Theatre: From Shamanistic Ritual to Contemporary Pluralism*. Revised ed. Princeton, NJ: Princeton University Press.

Papas, Alexandre. 2019. *Thus Spake the Dervish: Sufism, Language, and the Religious Margins in Central Asia, 1400–1900*. Leiden: Brill.

Peacock, Andrew. 2019. *Islam, Literature and Society in Mongol Anatolia*. *Islam, Literature and Society in Mongol Anatolia*. Cambridge: Cambridge University Press.

Pelliot, Paul. 1914. "La version ouigoure de l'histoire des princes Kalyāṇaṃkara et Pāpaṃkara." *T'oung Pao* 15(2), 225–72.

Pelliot, Paul. 1932. "Tokharien et Koutchéen." *Journal Asiatique* 224, 23–106.

Pian, Rulan Chao. 1967. *Sonq Dynasty Musical Sources and Their Interpretation*. Cambridge, MA: Harvard University Press.

Picken, Laurence. 1955. "The Origin of the Short Lute." *The Galpin Society Journal* 8, 32–42.

Picken, Laurence. 1969. "T'ang Music and Musical Instruments." *T'oung Pao* 55(1), 74–122.

Picken, Laurence. 1975. *Folk Musical Instruments of Turkey*. London: Oxford University Press.

Picken, Laurence, ed. 1985a. *Music from the Tang Court*, vol. 2. Cambridge: Cambridge University Press.

Picken, Laurence, ed. 1985b. *Music from the Tang Court*, vol. 3. Cambridge: Cambridge University Press.

Picken, Laurence, ed. 1987. *Music from the Tang Court*, vol. 4. Cambridge: Cambridge University Press.

Picken, Laurence, and Noël J. Nickson. 1997. *Music from the Tang Court*, vol. 6 Cambridge: Cambridge University Press.

Picken, Laurence, and Noël J. Nickson. 2000. *Music from the Tang Court 7: Some Ancient Connections Explored*. Cambridge: Cambridge University Press.

Puerta Vílchez, José Miguel. 2017. *Aesthetics in Arabic Thought: From Pre-Islamic Arabia through al-Andalus*. Leiden: Brill.

Qaddūmī, Ghāda Ḥijjāwī. 1996. *Book of Gifts and Rarities (Kitāb al-Hadāyā Wa al-Tuaf): Selections Compiled in the Fifteenth Century from an Eleventh Century Manuscript on Gifts and Treasures*. Cambridge, MA: Harvard University Press.

Raghavan, Venkataraman. 1952. *Yantras or Mechanical Contrivances in Ancient India*. Basavangudi, Bangalore: Indian Institute of Culture.

Rancier, Megan. 2014. "The Musical Instrument as National Archive: A Case Study of the Kazakh Qyl-Qobyz." *Ethnomusicology* 58(3), 379–404.

Rees, Helen. 2000. *Echoes of History: Naxi Music in Modern China*. Oxford: Oxford University Press.

Reichl, Karl. 1992. *Turkic Oral Epic Poetry: Tradition, Forms, Poetic Structure*. New York: Garland.

Rhie, Marylin Martin. 2002. *Early Buddhist Art of China and Central Asia*, vol. 2, *The Eastern Chin and Sixteen Kingdoms Period in China and Tumshuk, Kucha and Karashahr in Central Asia*. Leiden: Brill.

Rippa, Alessandro. 2014. "Re-Writing Mythology in Xinjiang: The Case of the Queen Mother of the West, King Mu and the Kunlun." *The China Journal* 71, 43–64.

Rong Xinjiang. 2018. "Sogdian Merchants and Sogdian Culture on the Silk Road." In *Empires and Exchanges in Eurasian Late Antiquity Rome, China, Iran, and the Steppe, ca. 250–750*, edited by Nicola di Cosmo and Michael Maas, 84–95. Cambridge: Cambridge University Press.

Rosenfield, John M. 1968. "A Note on Three Ancient Japanese Dance Masks." *Acquisitions (Fogg Art Museum)* 1968, 9–20.

Rothschild, Norman Harry. 2017. "*Sumozhe* Suppressed, *Huntuo* Halted: An Investigation into the Nature and Stakes of the Cold-Splashing Sogdian Festal Dramas Performed in Early Eighth Century Tang China." *Frontiers of History in China* 12(2), 262–300.

Saliba, George. 2015. "The Mysterious Provenance of Banū Mūsā's Treatise on Music." In *Allah's Automata: Artifacts of the Arab-Islamic Renaissance (800–1200)*, edited by Siegfried Zielinski and Peter Weibel, 58–64. Ostfildern: Hatje Cantz Verlag.

Samir, Imad. 2015. "Banū Mūsā ibn Shākir: A Programmable Universal Musical Automaton: Two Translations." In *Allah's Automata: Artifacts of the Arab-Islamic Renaissance (800–1200)*, edited by Siegfried Zielinski and Peter Weibel, 68–86. Ostfildern: Hatje Cantz Verlag.

Schaefer, Christiane. 2010. "Multilingualism and Language Contact in Urban Centres along the Silk Road during the First Millennium AD." In *The Urban Mind Cultural and Environmental Dynamics*, edited by Paul J. J. Sinclair, Gullög Nordquist, Frands Herschend, and Christian Isendahl, 441–55. Uppsala: Uppsala University.

Schafer, Edward H. 1963. *The Golden Peaches of Samarkand: A Study of T'ang Exotics*. Berkeley: University of California Press.

Scholz, Bernhard Walter. 1972. *Carolingian Chronicles: Royal Frankish Annals and Nithard's Histories*. Ann Arbor: University of Michigan Press.

Sha Wutian 沙武田. 2013. "Tangyun hufeng – Mogaoku di 220 ku wudaotu yu Chang'an fengqi 唐韵胡风 – 莫高窟第220窟舞蹈图与长安风气" [The dance scene in Mogao Cave 220 and fashions in Chang'an]. *Shaanxi lishi bowuguan guankan* 陕西历史博物馆馆刊 [*Bulletin of the Shaanxi History Museum*] 20, 189–205

Sha Wutian. 2016. "An Image of Nightime Music and Dance in Tang Chang'an: Notes on the Lighting Devices in the Medicine Buddha Transformation Tableau in Mogao Cave 220, Dunhuang." *The Silk Road* 14, 19–41.

Slavin, Philip. 2019. "Death by the Lake: Mortality Crisis in Early Fourteenth-Century Central Asia." *Journal of Interdisciplinary History* 50 (1), 59–90.

Star, Susan Leigh, and James R. Griesemer. 1989. "Institutional Ecology, 'Translations' and Boundary Objects: Amateurs and Professionals in

Berkeley's Museum of Vertebrate Zoology, 1907–39." *Social Studies of Science* 19(3), 387–420.

Sultanova, Razia. 2011. *From Shamanism to Sufism: Women, Islam and Culture in Central Asia.* London : I. B. Tauris.

Sun, Xiaojing. 2012. "The Sound of Silence: Daqu 大曲 ("Big-Suite") and Medieval Chinese Performance." PhD diss., University of California, Berkeley.

Tauer, Felix. 1934. "Continuation du Ẓafarnāma de Niẓāmuddin Šāmī par Ḥāfiẓ-i Abrū. Editée d'après les manuscrits de Stamboul." *Archiv Orientální* 6, 429–65.

Thilo, Thomas. 2006. *Chang'an: Metropole Ostasiens Und Weltstadt Des Mittelalte, Teil 2: Gesellschaft Und Kultur.* Wiesbaden: Otto Harrassowitz.

Trombert, Eric, and Étienne de la Vaissière, eds. 2005. *Les Sogdiens en Chine.* Paris: École française d'Extrême-Orient.

Truitt, E. R. 2015. *Medieval Robots: Mechanism, Magic, Nature, and Art.* Philadelphia: University of Pennsylvania Press.

Tsuge Gen'ichi. 2019. "Shidurghū: In Search of a Vanished Lute of the Timurid Period." *Studia Instrumentorum Musicae Popularis* (New Series) 6, 347–58.

Twitchett, Denis C., and Anthony H. Christie. 1959. "A Medieval Burmese Orchestra." *Asia Major* 7, 176–95.

Veselovskiy, Nikolai Ivanovich. 1915. "Sovremennoye sostoyaniye voprosa o 'Kamennykh Babakh' ili 'Balbalakh.'" *Zapiski Imperatorskogo Odesskogo Obshchestva Istorii i Drevnostey* 32, 408–44.

Vovin, Alexander, Edward Vajda, and Etienne de la Vassière. 2016. "Who Were the *Kjet (羯) and What Language Did They Speak?" *Journal Asiatique* 304.1, 125–44.

Waley, Arthur. 1949. *Life and Times of Po Chu-i.* New York: MacMillan.

Wang, Penglin. 1993. "On the Etymology of English Silk: A Case Study of IE and Altaic Contact." *Central Asiatic Journal* 37(3–4), 225–48.

Wang Xiaodun and Sun Xiaohui. 2004. "Yuebu of the Tang Dynasty: Musical Transmission from the Han to the Early Tang Dynasty." *Yearbook of Traditional Music* 36, 50–64.

Wang Zhenping. 2005. *Ambassadors from the Island of Immortals: China-Japan Relations in the Han-Tang Period.* Honolulu: Association for Asian Studies.

Wang-Toutain, Françoise. 1996. "Le sacre du printemps: Les cérémonies bouddhiques du 8e jour du 2e mois." In *De Dunhuang au Japon: etudes chinoises et bouddhiques offertes à Michel Soymié*, edited by Jean-Pierre Drège, 73–92. Geneva: Librairie Droz.

Watson, William. 1979. "Review of Ryoichi Hayashi, *The Silk Road and the Shoso-in*, tr. Robert Ricketts (New York: Weatherhill; Tokyo: Heibonsha, 1975)." *Bulletin of the School of Oriental and African Studies* 42(1), 167–68.

Watt, James C. Y., An Jiayao, Angela F. Howard, Boris I. Marshak, Su Bai, and Zhao Feng. 2004. *China: Dawn of the Golden Age, 200–750 AD*. New York: The Metropolitan Museum of Art/New Haven, CT: Yale University Press.

Watters, Thomas, ed. 1904. *On Yuan Chwang's Travels to India 629–645 A.D.* London: Royal Asiatic Society.

Wellesz, Egon. 1961. *A History of Byzantine Music and Hymnography*. Oxford: Clarendon Press.

Whitfield, Susan, ed. 2019. *Silk Roads: Peoples, Cultures, Landscapes*. London: Thames and Hudson.

Widdess, Richard. 1995. *The Ragas of Early Indian Music: Modes, Melodies, and Musical Notations from the Gupta Period to c. 1250*. Oxford: Clarendon Press.

Wilkens, Jens. 2015. "Buddhism in the West Uyghur Kingdom and Beyond." In *Transfer of Buddhism Across Central Asian Networks (7th to 13th Centuries)*, edited by Carmen Meinert, 189–249. Leiden: Brill.

William of Rubruck. 1990. *The Mission of Friar William of Rubruck: His Journey to the Court of the Great Khan Mongke, 1253–1255*, edited by Peter Jackson and David Morgan. London: Hakluyt Society.

Wu Hung. 2020. "Thinking Through Scale: The First Emperor's Sculptural Enterprise." In *Figurines: Figuration and The Sense of Scale*, edited by Jaś Elsner, 88–129. Oxford: Oxford University Press.

Xuanzang. 1996. *The Great Tang Dynasty Record of the Western Regions*, translated by Li Rongxi. Berkeley: Numata Center for Buddhist Translation & Research.

Yan, Hong-Sen, and Tsung-Yi Lin. 2002. "A Study on Ancient Chinese Time Laws and the Time-Telling System of Su Song's Clock Tower." *Mechanism and Machine Theory* 37(1), 15–33.

Yang Yinliu 楊蔭瀏. *Zhongguo gudai yinyue shigao* 中國古代音樂史稿 [*Draft History of Ancient Chinese Music*], vol. 2. Taipei: Danqing tushu youxian gongsi, 1985.

Yao Shihong 姚士宏. 1983–1985. "Kejiru sekkutsu hekiga no gakubu keishō キジル石窟壁画の楽舞形象 [Musical Instruments and Dancing Depicted as They Appear in Wall Paintings at the Kizil Grottoes]." In *Kijiru Sekkutsu* キジル石窟壁画 [*The Caves of Kizil*] by Shinkyō Uiguru Jichiku Bunbutsu Kanri Iinkai 新疆ウイクル自治区文物管理委員会 [Xinjiang Uighur Autonomous Region Committee for Cultural Relics] and Haijōken Kijiru

Senbutsudō Bunbutsu Hokanjo 拝城県キジル千仏洞窟文物保管所 [Baicheng-xian Kizil Thousand Buddha Caves Cultural Relics Preservation Center], 237–57. *Chūgoku sekkutsu* 中国石窟 [*The Grottoes of China*], vol. 2. Tokyo: Heibonsha.

Yatsenko, Sergey. 2012. "Sogdian Costume in Chinese and Sogdian Art of the 6th–8th Centuries." In *Serica – Da Qin Studies in Archaeology, Philology and History of Sino-Western Relations (Selected Problems)*, edited by Gościwit Malinowski, Aleksander Paroń, and Bartłomiej Sz. Szmoniewski, 101–14. Wrocław: Wrocław University.

Zeng Jinshou. 2003. "Chinas Musik und Musikerziehung im kulturellen Austausch mit den Nachbarländern und dem Westen." PhD diss., University of Bremen.

Zhalmaganbetov, Zhalgas, Zainolla Samashev, and Ulan Umitkaliev. 2015. "Ancient Musicians' Monuments in the Kazakh Altai." *Anthropologist* 22 (3), 545–52.

Zhang Qingjie. 2005. "Hutengwu and Huxuanwu: Sogdian Dances in the Northern, Sui and Tang Dynasties." In *Les Sogdiens En Chine*, edited by Eric Trombert and Étienne de la Vaissière, 93–106. Paris: École française d'Extrême-Orient.

Zheng Zuxiang 鄭祖襄. 2000. "Zai Tan 'Xijing Zaji' de 'Fanyu Zhi Yue' 再談 《西京雜記》的'璠璵之樂.' [Discussing Again the "Music of the Fanyu" in the *Miscellaneous Records of the Western Capital*]" *Yinyue Yishu* 音樂藝術 [*The Art of Music*] 3, 14–16.

Zürcher, Erik. 1990. "Han Buddhism and the Western Regions." In *Thought and Law in Qin and Han China: Studies Dedicated to Anthony Hulsewé on the Occasion of His Eightieth Birthday*, edited by Erik Zürcher, Idema Wilk Lukas, and Anthony Hulsewe, 158–82. Leiden: Brill.

Zürcher, Erik. 2007. *The Buddhist Conquest of China: The Spread and Adaptation of Buddhism in Early Medieval China*. 3rd ed. Leiden: Brill.

Cambridge Elements ≡

The Global Middle Ages

Geraldine Heng
University of Texas at Austin

Geraldine Heng is Perceval Professor of English and Comparative Literature at the University of Texas, Austin. She is the author of *The Invention of Race in the European Middle Ages* (2018) and *England and the Jews: How Religion and Violence Created the First Racial State in the West* (2018), both published by Cambridge University Press, as well as *Empire of Magic: Medieval Romance and the Politics of Cultural Fantasy* (2003, Columbia). She is the editor of *Teaching the Global Middle Ages* (2022, MLA), coedits the University of Pennsylvania Press series, RaceB4Race: Critical Studies of the Premodern, and is working on a new book, *Early Globalisms: The Interconnected World, 500–1500 CE*. Originally from Singapore, Heng is a Fellow of the Medieval Academy of America, a member of the Medievalists of Color, and Founder and Co-director, with Susan Noakes, of the Global Middle Ages Project: www.globalmiddleages.org.

Susan Noakes
University of Minnesota, Twin Cities

Susan Noakes is Professor and Chair of French and Italian at the University of Minnesota, Twin Cities. From 2002 to 2008 she was Director of the Center for Medieval Studies; she has also served as Director of Italian Studies, Director of the Center for Advanced Feminist Studies, and Associate Dean for Faculty in the College of Liberal Arts. Her publications include *The Comparative Perspective on Literature: Essays in Theory and Practice* (coedited with Clayton Koelb, Cornell, 1988) and *Timely Reading: Between Exegesis and Interpretation* (Cornell, 1988), along with many articles and critical editions in several areas of French, Italian, and neo-Latin Studies. She is the Founder and Co-director, with Geraldine Heng, of the Global Middle Ages Project: www.globalmiddleages.org.

About the Series

Elements in the Global Middle Ages is a series of concise studies that introduce researchers and instructors to an uncentered, interconnected world, c. 500-1500 CE. Individual Elements focus on the globe's geographic zones, its natural and built environments, its cultures, societies, arts, technologies, peoples, ecosystems, and lifeworlds.

Cambridge Elements ≡

The Global Middle Ages

Elements in the Series

A full series listing is available at: www.cambridge.org/EGMA

Printed in the United States
by Baker & Taylor Publisher Services